Anyone for Breakfast?

A comedy

Derek Benfield

Samuel French — London
New York - Toronto - Hollywood

ANYONE FOR BREAKFAST?

First presented at the SchaterTeater in Antwerp on 7th December 1991, with the following cast:

Shirley	Simonne Peeters
Jane	Janine Bischops
Mark	Guido de Craene
Gilbert	Walter Van de Velde
Helga	Griet Naessens
Roger	Johny Voners

Directed by Marnix Verduyn
Setting by Jan Verstraeten

Subsequently presented at the Contra-Kreis Theater, Bonn, on 3rd December 1992, with the following cast:

Shirley	Anne Springmann
Jane	Sibylle Nicolai
Mark	Robert Jarczyk
Gilbert	Rainer Delventhal
Helga	Jutta Grobkinsky
Roger	Karl Heinz Fiege

Directed by Horst Johanning
Setting by Pit Fischer

The action takes place in Shirley's and Gilbert's country house

ACT I	A Friday evening in the winter
ACT II	The next morning

Time — the present

Other plays by Derek Benfield published by
Samuel French Ltd:

Bedside Manners
Beyond a Joke
A Bird in the Hand
Caught on the Hop
Don't Lose the Place!
Fish Out of Water
Flying Feathers
In for the Kill
Look Who's Talking!
Murder for the Asking
Off the Hook!
Panic Stations
Post Horn Gallop
Running Riot
A Toe in the Water
Touch and Go
Wild Goose Chase

ACT I

The living-room of Shirley and Gilbert's country house. A Friday evening in the winter

The curtains are drawn and the lights are on

The room is tastefully decorated and the furniture is comfortable and expensive. There is a staircase R up to a landing which goes off left and right. A door DR leads to the dining-room, an archway DL to the hall and front door, and another door UL to the kitchen. There are french windows in the back wall with built-in cupboards and shelves R of them on which stand various books and ornaments. Against the side of the staircase is a desk with a lamp and a silver framed photograph of Gilbert, and a wastepaper basket below the desk. A sofa stands C with a narrow table above it and a lamp on a coffee table to the L. There is a small low armchair DRC with a drinks trolley above it. In the corner UL is an oak chest. Below the kitchen door are recessed shelves and a cupboard on which the stereo system stands. A telephone and a light dimmer switch are on the wall above the archway. There are a few potted house plants here and there

An open travel bag is on the sofa with various items including a towel and a washbag lying nearby. Shirley's coat is on the back of the sofa. The theme music before the play begins will continue after the CURTAIN rises until the dialogue starts

Shirley walks in briskly from the dining-room, looking for something. She is a pretty, energetic woman in her forties. She opens and closes the cupboards near the windows, searching frantically. Not finding what she wants, she runs across to search in the cupboard under the stereo system

Jane comes downstairs with far less energy. She is about the same age as Shirley and attractive, but at present rather unsure of herself. She is wearing a red dress that is perhaps a little too flamboyant for her, and about which she is obviously self-conscious. She moves into the room, considering the garment's suitability. The music stops

Jane Shirley ...

Shirley (*searching; desperately*) I can't find it anywhere!

Jane (*her mind on her dress*) What?

Shirley I had it last Friday when I'd finished with it! (*She disappears head-first into the cupboard to look*)

Jane Shirley ...

Shirley (*her head inside the cupboard*) Hmm?

Jane What do you think?

Shirley (*emerging from the cupboard*) Sorry? (*She sees the dress and laughs a little*) Is *that* what you're wearing?

Jane (*rather hurt*) What's wrong with it?

Shirley Oh, nothing! Nothing at all!

Jane You don't like it.

Shirley Yes, I do! It's very nice. Very nice indeed. Definitely makes a statement.

Jane Well, I didn't know *what* to wear! I've never done this sort of thing before.

Shirley Haven't you?

Jane You know very well I haven't!

Shirley Well, I expect you'll soon get into the swing of it. (*She indicates the dress reassuringly*) It's very nice. Really. It must be here somewhere ... (*Her head disappears into the cupboard again*)

Jane (*studying her dress without enthusiasm*) Where do you *usually* put it?

Shirley (*emerging again*) Sorry?

Jane Where do you usually put it on a Friday when you've finished with it? (*She sits down in the armchair to see how the dress looks in a sitting position*)

Shirley In my bag, of course. But it's not there.

Jane Couldn't you manage without it for once?

Shirley Are you mad? Fine sight I'd be rolling about on the floor without one! (*She goes on to her hands and knees to look under the sofa*)

Jane It wouldn't have ended up under there, surely?

Shirley (*peering under the sofa*) You never know!

Jane slumps in the armchair, dispiritedly, unimpressed by the dress's performance, and sinks her face into her hand despondently

(*Finding nothing*) Oh, blast! Now where the hell can ...? Ah! I know!

(*She starts to go and sees Jane deep in gloom*) For heaven's sake, cheer up! He'll be here in a minute! (*She runs towards the stairs*)

Jane I'm not sure that this is a good idea ...

Shirley (*hesitating*) What?

Jane Well ... he's quite a bit younger than I am.

Shirley (*grinning with delight*) You mean you've got yourself a toy-boy?

Jane (*gloomily*) Yes. I suppose I have ...

Shirley Well, think yourself lucky! Most women here in Little Bendon would give their eye-teeth for a toy-boy.

Jane You don't think he'll guess why I asked him here, do you?

Shirley Oh, I think that dress might give him a rough idea!

She laughs and runs off up the stairs at high speed

Jane gets up and wanders away a little, like a model on a catwalk, to see if the dress looks better when in motion

(*Off*) Aaaah!

Shirley reappears and runs downstairs, breathlessly waving a bright-coloured leotard in the air

Got it!

Jane Where was it?

Shirley In the airing cupboard. (*She hastens to the sofa to put the leotard in her travel bag*) Thank heaven for that! I could hardly turn up for my aerobics class without my leotard, could I? (*Packing the rest of her things and zipping up the travel bag*) Now, you know where everything is, don't you? The food's in the dining-room and the bedroom's upstairs!

Jane Food?

Shirley You are going to *eat* first, aren't you?

Jane Oh — oh, yes! Yes, of course! (*Embarrassed, she escapes back to the armchair*)

Shirley (*putting on lipstick*) You mustn't let him think you're too keen, you know. I hope you're not going to leap on him the minute he walks through the front door.

Jane (*appalled at the thought*) Of course I'm not!

Shirley That's all right, then. First impressions are very important. (*Teasing her*) Just because you're dressed in red doesn't mean you have to behave like some tart from Montmartre.

But Jane, lacking in confidence, is hardly the picture of a femme fatale

You've got to ... ease into it gradually. (*She puts away her lipstick*)

Jane If we're going to eat first I won't have *time* to ease into it gradually. When will you be back?

Shirley Don't worry! I'll telephone first to see how you're getting on. (*She puts on her coat*)

Jane (*sulking a little*) I won't be getting on at all if you ring up in the middle of it ...

Shirley (*as to a novice*) Jane ... if he's still here you don't answer it.

Jane Don't I?

Shirley Of course not! You really *haven't* done this before, have you! I'll hang on for four rings. All right? And if I get no reply after four I'll assume the best and stay the night with a friend. (*She collects her travel bag from the sofa*)

Jane (*losing heart*) No!!

Shirley What's the matter?

Jane It's no good. I can't go through with it! (*She darts towards the stairs*)

Shirley grabs her and they struggle a little

Shirley You can't change your mind *now*! He'll already be on his way! You did say you fancied him on the squash court.

Jane Yes. But he was running about there.

Shirley Well, he'll probably be running about here! Now, there's a bottle of champagne in the fridge. I got it specially. That should get things going. Right! I'm off! Have a nice time! (*She starts to go*)

Jane Shirley —!

Shirley (*putting on the brakes*) Now what?

Jane (*embarrassed*) I don't need to tell Mark that this is *your* house, do I? I wouldn't want him to think that I'm a loose woman who's borrowed a friend's house for a secret assignation.

Shirley But you *are* — and you *have*!

Jane Yes — *you* know that — and *I* know that, but I don't want *him* to know that, do I?

Shirley All right — do what you like. But remember — whatever happens, Gilbert mustn't find out about tonight. I don't think he'd approve. He's a very moral man, my husband.

Jane Is he?

Shirley You know very well he is! Now what about Roger?

Jane Sorry?

Shirley Don't say you've forgotten your husband already!

Jane No, of course not! He's at home tonight. Watching the football.

Shirley Oh, good. And where does *he* think *you* are?

Jane At my old school reunion. (*She giggles at her own bravado*) And that always goes on for hours, so he won't be waiting up for me.

Shirley So you see? You've got *plenty* of time to ease into it. (*She starts to go, and then turns back, remembering something else*) And if Gilbert rings, don't tell him what you're doing here!

Jane (*apprehensively*) He *won't* ring, will he?

Shirley He might. He often does when he's away in Germany. It's funny that. He never rings if he's in Darlington or Dewsbury. Only if he's in Düsseldorf. I expect he feels cut off by the English Channel. Makes him feel homesick. Either that or he's got a guilty conscience about something. (*Encouragingly*) For heaven's sake, cheer up! Everything's going to be all right. You're going to have a lovely evening. (*She waves*) *Ciao!*

Jane Bye ...

Shirley goes into the hall. The front door slams

But Jane is not the confident femme fatale she would like to be. She glances at her wrist-watch anxiously, then she notices the drinks trolley and hastens to it. She pours a hefty whisky and drinks it down in one. Then she realizes she may now smell of whisky and races to her handbag, takes out a small breath freshener and sprays her mouth twice. She puts away the freshener. Emboldened a little by the whisky, Jane goes about the room making sure everything is to her liking. She tidies a cushion on the sofa, adjusts the position of a table. She looks about, thinks the lights are a bit bright, notices the light switch and goes and turns down the dimmer. The Lights fade slightly. She smiles, better pleased. She decides to turn on the stereo. Very loud, noisy music blasts out and makes her jump. She quickly re-tunes it to play romantic string music. She half-heartedly essays a few dance steps, then stops and adjusts her dress to show a little more cleavage

She is far from pleased with the result, gives a sigh and goes out into the dining-room to check on the food

The kitchen door opens slowly and a helmeted figure in black leather motorbike gear comes in, tentatively, carrying a plastic bag. This is Mark, a good-looking young man in his late twenties

Jane returns from the dining-room, sees the helmeted figure standing in the kitchen doorway, and screams loudly

Mark (*muffled*) It's only me! (*He takes off the helmet*)

Jane Mark! You gave me such a fright! (*Gazing at his clothes in wonder*) You didn't say you'd be travelling by motorbike. I never heard you arriving.

Mark I didn't want to disturb the neighbours. It's a bit noisy, you see. So I stopped at the end of the drive and pushed it.

Jane Well, you could have rung the doorbell. I wasn't expecting you to appear out of the kitchen. I thought you were a burglar!

Mark (*smiling; sheepishly*) Well, I didn't like to come to the front door in my boots, so I left the bike round the back. And the kitchen door was open, so I — I'm sorry if I made you jump.

Jane Never mind. You're here. That's the main thing. Let me take your hat. (*She takes his helmet*)

Mark It was lucky that I did.

Jane Sorry?

Mark Push my bike. Because somebody drove away in a hell of a hurry just as I was arriving.

Jane D-did they?

Mark A *lady* driver! Going too fast, if you ask me. We might have had a collision if I'd been *on* my bike instead of pushing it.

Jane Ah — yes — of course! That would be the cleaning lady!

Mark At this time of night?

Jane She's a very slow worker. Takes her simply ages to do the kitchen floor. Aren't you going to take them off?

Mark Eh?

Jane Surely you're not going to spend the whole evening standing about in leather?

Mark (*realizing*) Oh. Yes. Right.

Jane I'll hang your hat in the hall.

She takes his helmet into the hall

Mark proceeds to take off his boots, his leather trousers and then his jacket, putting the items in a neat pile on the floor

Jane returns and watches him with growing astonishment

It is gradually revealed that Mark is wearing a dinner suit with black tie. From the plastic bag he produces a pair of evening shoes and puts them on. He is now immaculate. He smiles at her triumphantly

Good heavens! You needn't have dressed up. It's quite informal.
Mark Well ... you did say dinner, so I wasn't sure, was I? Dinner in the country could have been a party.
Jane Well, it isn't! It's just the two of us.
Mark Oh ...
Jane I thought you realized that.
Mark No ...

Jane's meagre confidence receives a further blow

Jane I do hate being the subject of an anti-climax. (*She moves towards him*) When I asked you to come to dinner, I — (*she trips over his pile of discarded clothing*) Oh, damn ...! (*She gathers them up*) I'll put these out of the way, shall I? I don't want to trip over them every time I make a move. (*She moves towards the hall*)
Mark (*watching her go; with a smile*) Anyhow, *you* look as if you're dressed for a party!
Jane Do I? (*She looks down at her dress as if seeing it for the first time*) Oh, *this*! (*She smiles hopefully*) Do you ... do you like it?
Mark It's very red ...
Jane (*deflated*) Yes, it is, isn't it ...? I hadn't noticed. I just slipped into the first thing that came to hand!

She scuttles out into the hall with his clothes

Mark glances around admiringly

Mark (*calling*) Nice place you've got here!

Jane returns

Jane Sorry?

Mark Nice house.

Jane Yes.

Mark How long have you lived here?

Jane Me? (*Quickly*) Ah — *me*! Yes! Er — not very long ...

Mark Must get lonely in the winter. All on your own in this big house.

Jane Oh, the neighbours are very friendly. Always popping in and out.

Mark You should have asked some of them tonight. I like meeting people.
  (*He smiles, socially*)

Jane (*rather disappointed by his lack of desire to be alone with her*) I ...
  I didn't think of it. I've only catered for two. (*She remembers her
  manners*) Would you like to sit down?

Mark Oh. Thanks. (*He sits on the sofa*)

Jane Can I get you a drink? You ... you do *drink*, I hope?

Mark Oh, yes.

Jane Oh, good! (*Impressively*) There's a bottle of champagne in the fridge
  ... (*she moves towards the kitchen*)

Mark I thought champagne was only for special occasions.

Jane (*stopping; doing her best to bear this unintended rebuff with
  fortitude*) That's what I thought this *was*!

Mark I'd prefer a beer.

Jane A *beer*? (*Quietly*) That's not going to get things going ...

Mark Sorry?

Jane (*covering; hastily*) I don't think they've got any — er — I don't think
  I've got any! (*Fed up*) I'll have a look in the fridge. (*She starts to go
  again*)

Mark Jane ——

Jane (*stopping; hopefully*) Yes?

Mark (*with a smile*) This music's a bit old-fashioned, isn't it?

Jane Is it? (*She feels a hundred years old*) Oh ... (*She switches off the
  stereo abruptly*)

She goes into the kitchen

Mark glances around and notices the framed photograph of Gilbert on the desk. He peers at it, but it is a little far away in the dim light

Jane (*off*) There's a can of lager! That any good?
Mark (*calling*) Great!

Jane returns, peering at a can of lager

Jane I don't think it's past its drink-by date ... (*She hands it to him*)
Mark Ta. (*He opens the can with a report like a pistol shot*)
Jane (*jumping*) Aah!
Mark (*grinning at her*) You *are* nervous, aren't you?
Jane Just a little, yes ...
Mark Aren't *you* having anything?
Jane Well ... perhaps I'll have just a *very* small scotch. (*She hastens to pour herself a not very small whisky and, with her back to him, downs it in one*)
Mark (*raising his can*) Cheers!
Jane Cheers! (*She raises her glass*)

They both notice that her glass is already empty. She gives an embarrassed smile. "Funny lady", he thinks — and drinks from his can. Jane puts down her empty glass and turns to him

   (*Abruptly*) Nuts?
Mark (*spluttering as he nearly chokes on his drink*) Sorry?
Jane I'll go and find you some nuts. Young men always like nuts. (*She moves towards the kitchen*)
Mark Jane ——
Jane (*stopping; hopefully*) Yes?
Mark Bit ... dark in here, isn't it?
Jane Is it? I hadn't noticed.

She bangs the lights back up to full and goes into the kitchen

Mark gets up, puts his lager down on the drinks trolley and goes to get a closer look at the photograph of Gilbert. He picks it up so he can read the message written on it, then puts it down again, now clearly a very worried man

Jane returns with a dish of nuts

She goes to him and sees the severe look he is giving her

Jane *Now* what's the matter?
Mark I didn't know that you were married ...

Jane holds his look for a moment, then proffers the dish of nuts

Jane Nuts?
Mark You never said that you were married!
Jane I didn't think you'd want to know. At the squash club you seemed to be interested in *me*, not my husband ... (*She puts the nuts down on the sofa table*) How did you *know* I was married?

Mark picks up the photograph and holds it aloft

   Oh, my God! I didn't know *that* was there ...!
Mark This *is* your husband?
Jane No!
Mark What?
Jane I can explain — !
Mark There's nothing to explain. (*He reads*) "To my darling wife — from Gilbert". There it is — for all the world to see!
Jane Well, not *all* the world. Just a few people from Little Bendon ...
Mark If you're a married woman why are you inviting young men home for dinner?
Jane You're only *one* young man ...
Mark One young man's quite enough for a married woman!
Jane Yes — that's what *I* thought. That's why I didn't invite the neighbours.
Mark (*waving the photograph at her*) What would Gilbert think?
Jane I don't think Gilbert would mind ...! Mark ... I thought you *wanted* to come to dinner. That was the impression you gave me at the squash club. (*Moving away from him despondently*) I've got cold salmon and Chablis in the dining-room ...
Mark (*following her; wildly*) I didn't know then that you were happily married to Gilbert!
Jane I'm not!

Mark What?

Jane (*truthfully*) Gilbert and I are not happily married.

Mark stares at her for a moment, then he sighs sympathetically, thinking he has stumbled upon the truth

Mark Oh — I *see* ...! I'm sorry — I should have realized. Gilbert treated you badly! Is that it?

Jane (*assuming the attitude of a woman who has suffered*) Oh, Mark — how did you *guess*?!

Mark encloses her in his comforting arms, which she enjoys

Mark There, there ...! (*He has second thoughts and pulls away*) But if he treated you badly, why do you still keep his photograph?

Jane Give that to me! (*She grabs the photograph, moves away and whispers to it*) Sorry, Gilbert ... (*She throws it with abandon into the wastepaper basket*) I don't want to see Gilbert's face ever again! (*She looks triumphantly at Mark*) There! Everything all right *now*?

Mark (*enthusiastically*) You bet! Let's get on with it, shall we?

Jane I thought you'd never ask ...! (*She returns to him with renewed optimism*)

Mark Shall we start now?

Jane Anytime you like!

Mark I don't often have it, you know.

Jane Don't you?

Mark It's quite a treat for me, I can tell you.

Jane It's quite a treat for me, too ...!

Mark I don't get it every day of the week, you know.

Jane Neither do I!

Mark In fact, I can't remember the last time I had cold salmon and Chablis.

Jane Oh. You do want to *eat*, then?

Mark Well, I am rather hungry.

Jane So am I. (*Quietly*) But not for cold salmon and Chablis ...

Mark What?

Jane Never mind! (*She picks up her handbag*) Come on! The dining-room's through here. (*As she goes*) You can eat first — and *then* try to work up an appetite!

Mark looks puzzled by this as he follows Jane into the dining-room, closing the door behind them

The front door slams and, after a moment, Gilbert comes in from the hall with his raincoat on. He is a good-looking, amiable man in his forties. He looks about and then goes back to call to somebody in the hall

Gilbert It's all right. Come on in.

A delightfully pretty girl with good legs comes in. She is in the uniform of a Lufthansa air hostess. This is Helga

Helga You are quite sure she is out?

Gilbert (*removing his raincoat*) I told you. Shirley goes to her aerobics class on a Friday. She won't be back for ages.

Helga But the lights are all on.

Gilbert She always leaves them on when she's out. Thinks it fools prospective burglars into thinking there's someone at home.

He takes his coat out into the hall

Helga (*looking about approvingly*) Hmm. Very nice.

Gilbert returns

Gilbert Glad you like it.

Helga (*sadly*) But I never thought we would be *here* tonight ...

Gilbert No. Neither did I.

They go into each other's arms, unhappily

Gilbert }
Helga } (*together*) Oooooo ...!

Helga We should have been together in Düsseldorf by now.

Gilbert Yes. I know. And I wish we were. They never said anything about fog on the radio. I don't think those forecasters know anything at all! They might just as well hang out a bit of seaweed.

Helga How long have we got?

Gilbert Sorry?

Helga Before your wife comes back.

Gilbert Oh — a couple of hours, I suppose.

Helga Then we had better get on with it! (*She sits on the sofa and starts unbuttoning her jacket*)

Gilbert (*alarmed*) What are you doing?

Helga Taking my clothes off.

Gilbert You can't do that! Not in *here*.

Helga You aren't expecting visitors, are you?

Gilbert Of course I'm not! But I ... I thought we'd have an aperitif first.

Helga I do not need an aperitif ... (*She unfastens some more buttons*)

Gilbert Well, *I* do! (*He fastens up her buttons again*)

Helga (*smiling at him sexily*) Don't tell me you're shy? You're never shy when we are in Düsseldorf ...

Gilbert That's different. There's sea between here and Düsseldorf. Miles of it. And in Düsseldorf we're in a hotel. This is my sitting-room. You can't take your clothes off in my sitting-room!

Helga Come on, then!

She grabs his hand and starts to drag him towards the stairs

Gilbert Where are we going?

Helga Upstairs. You must have a room upstairs where I can take my clothes off.

Gilbert (*resisting manfully*) Couldn't we have a drink first?

Helga (*reluctantly*) Oh — very well. Drinks first. *Then* afters.

Gilbert Good! What would you like?

Helga We usually have champagne.

Gilbert I don't think we've got any of that. (*He notices the lager can*) Good Lord ...

Helga What?

Gilbert (*picking up the lager can*) I didn't know my wife was a secret lager lout. No wonder she goes to exercise classes. Right! Let's see what we can find in the fridge. (*He sets off towards the kitchen with the lager can, puzzled by its presence*)

Helga (*as they go*) But Gilbert, don't let's waste *too* much time drinking ...

They disappear into the kitchen, closing the door behind them

Mark and Jane look in from the dining-room. They both have white table napkins tucked in at their necks

Jane There you are, you see? What did I tell you?

Mark Well, I could have sworn I heard voices ...

Jane See for yourself! There's nobody here. Just the two of us. (*Wearily*) Mark, let's go back to the dining-room — and do try to concentrate on *me* ...

Mark (*miles away*) What?

Jane Well, if that's too difficult, for heaven's sake focus on the fish!

She pulls him back inside and closes the door

Gilbert and Helga look in from the kitchen. He is carrying a bottle of champagne and two glasses

Helga There you are, you see? What did I tell you?

Gilbert Well, I could have sworn I heard voices ...

Helga See for yourself, liebling! There's nobody here. Just the two of us.

Gilbert Yes, I suppose so ... (*He puts the glasses on the drinks trolley*)

Helga (*putting her arms around him*) I hope you are not just pretending to hear voices ...

Gilbert Don't be silly! Why should I do that? (*He starts opening the bottle behind her back*)

Helga Perhaps you are frightened of being alone with me in your own house ...

Gilbert I brought you here, didn't I?

Helga Only because you had not left your car at the airport and I gave you a lift!

Gilbert Don't be silly, Helga. I *wanted* you to be here.

Helga Did you?

Gilbert Of course.

Helga Oh, liebling ...

She kisses him and (apparently as a result) the cork pops out of the bottle

You see — you *did* have champagne!

Gilbert Yes, I did, didn't I? I can't understand that ...

Helga Perhaps your wife bought it to surprise you.

Gilbert But it's not my birthday till September. (*He pours two glasses of champagne*)

Helga You don't suppose she put it there for a special occasion?

Gilbert Well, it's too late now. I've opened it. (*He hands a glass of champagne to her*) Well, here's to ...

Helga (*romantically*) To Düsseldorf ...!

Gilbert To Düsseldorf ...

They clink glasses and drink. Helga finishes hers off in one and then smiles at Gilbert enthusiastically

Helga Good! *Now* can we go upstairs, please? (*She starts to go*)

Gilbert Helga ...!

Helga Well, we have had our aperitif.

Gilbert You've had yours. I'm still drinking mine.

Helga Hurry up, then!

Gilbert You're supposed to sip champagne. (*He sits on the sofa and sips elegantly*)

Helga Well, sip it, then. But sip it quickly!

Gilbert Don't you want food first?

Helga (*pathetically*) But if we have aperitif *and* food we will not have time for anything else. You do *want* something else, don't you?

Gilbert Yes, darling — of course I do!

Helga Come on, then!

Gilbert But we haven't finished the champagne yet!

Helga We can finish the champagne upstairs. (*She picks up the bottle and heads for the stairs*)

Gilbert (*jumping up anxiously*) Helga!

Helga Then we can have aperitif and afters, both at the same time. (*She smiles delightfully and goes up the stairs*)

Gilbert But Helga — !

Helga Turn out the lights, liebling. I will be upstairs waiting for you ...

She smiles at him provocatively and goes off to the bedrooms

Gilbert (*moving after her*) No, Helga, I — I —— (*he dithers uncertainly, divided between his natural desires and his sensibilities*) Oh well — I did *try* ...

He notices something in the wastepaper basket. He bends down to retrieve his photograph. Deeply insulted, he dusts it off with his sleeve and replaces it in its usual position on the desk

He smiles, better pleased, and goes into the kitchen, closing the door behind him

As the kitchen door closes, the dining-room door opens and Mark comes in urgently, with Jane behind him. They still have the napkins tucked in at their necks. Jane is deeply frustrated

Mark I tell you, I heard it again!

Jane This isn't very flattering, you know.

Mark Sorry?

Jane You're sitting in the dining-room with a beautiful salmon and a not exactly repulsive woman and you're not paying any attention to either of us! All you're doing is listening to non-existent voices in the sitting-room!

Mark Might be burglars.

Jane If there are burglars what are they doing standing about gossiping when they should be pinching the silver?

Mark I'd better have a look ...

Jane Well, *I'm* going to finish my fish! You know, you're doing dreadful things to my self-confidence. After tonight I shall probably need psychiatric help!

She goes back into the dining-room, slamming the door noisily

Mark starts to move cautiously towards the kitchen, removing the napkin from his neck

Gilbert comes racing out of the kitchen (having heard the door slam) and stops in his tracks as he sees a total stranger dressed in a dinner jacket standing in the sitting-room

Mark stares at Gilbert, equally astonished

Gilbert }
Mark   } (*overlapping*) Who the hell are you?

Gilbert No, no — I started first! Who are you and why are you standing in the sitting-room?

Mark I'm ... I'm visiting.

Gilbert Well, you're wasting your time. I'm out.

Mark What?

Gilbert Well, I was *going* to be out. But there was fog, you see? At the airport. Thick fog. That's why I'm here and not there.

Mark Not where?

Gilbert Düsseldorf. (*He sighs, regretfully*) Oh, I wish I — (*He breaks off*) Are you a burglar?

Mark No, I'm not!

Gilbert Ah. No. Too well-dressed.

Mark (*nodding; wisely*) I *thought* I heard voices ...

Gilbert (*alarmed*) Where?

Mark In here! Just now!

Gilbert Ah — yes — that would be me!

Mark Sounded like *two* voices.

Gilbert Did it? (*He prowls away below the sofa*) Well, I was talking to myself. I often do that. When I'm alone. I have quite interesting conversations sometimes. If you're not a burglar, what the hell are you doing here?

Mark joins him a little uncertainly, unconsciously draping the napkin over his arm

Mark I ... I've come for dinner.

Gilbert (*noticing the napkin*) Oh, I see! You're from the "Dial-a-Waiter" service! Well, you must have been given the wrong address. There's no dinner party going on here.

Gilbert pushes Mark towards the hall. Mark resists, furiously

Mark I'm not a waiter! (*He throws the table napkin aside*)

Gilbert Then why are you dressed like that? Are you in an orchestra? Play the flute or something?

Mark No.

Gilbert Violin?

Mark No!

Gilbert Bassoon?

Mark No!!

Gilbert Ah! You're the conductor! (*He conducts briefly*)

Mark I'm nothing to do with an orchestra!

Gilbert Then what are you doing in my house?

Mark (*turning white*) *Your* house?

Gilbert Yes. My house. (*Indicating*) My sitting-room. My front door. (*Taking out his latchkey*) My latchkey. That's how I got in. How did *you* get in?

Mark You ... you *live* here?

Gilbert You're not slow on the uptake, I'll say that for you.

Mark (*with sudden agitation*) Wait a minute — ! You're not — ?

Mark hastens to the wastepaper basket and searches for the framed photograph. He does not find it, then sees that it is back in its usual position. He picks it up and peers at it closely, comparing it with the man before him. Then he points at it

Is ... this ... *you*?

Gilbert (*smiling pleasantly*) Yes.

Mark abruptly throws the photograph into the wastepaper basket and glares at Gilbert aggressively

Oh. Don't you like it?

Mark No, I don't!

Gilbert What a pity. I thought it was rather good of me.

Mark I don't like *any* of your photographs!

Gilbert (*hurt*) You can't say that.

Mark Why not?

Gilbert You've only seen *one*. I've got lots of photographs. I'll look them out, if you like. We're bound to find *one* that you approve of. I know! There's one of me taken in front of the pyramids sitting on a camel with a large banana in my hand. That might appeal to you.

Mark It won't!

Gilbert You can't be sure.

Mark I don't want to look at your photographs!

Gilbert Well, I think that's very rude. If I wandered into *your* house uninvited and you got out your photographs, I'd have the good manners to show some interest. (*He picks up the telephone receiver*)

Mark What are you doing?

Gilbert Calling the police.

Mark You don't have to do that!

Gilbert Oh yes, I do. We're not very keen on burglars in Little Bendon.

Mark I'm not a burglar!

Gilbert I've only got your word for that, haven't I? You've probably got a sackful of silver out in the dining-room. (*He replaces the receiver*) I'd better have a look. (*He moves towards the dining-room*)

Mark (*panicking and racing across to intercept him*) No! There's nothing in there!

Gilbert No swag?

Mark No! I didn't come here for that!

Gilbert Then what *did* you come here for?

Mark gathers himself to declare the truth and glares at Gilbert aggressively

Mark If you really want to know ——

Gilbert I do!

Mark I came here to have dinner with your wife!

Gilbert Bit of a wasted journey for you, then, wasn't it? Friday night's her aerobics night. Didn't she tell you that?

Mark (*puzzled*) Aerobics night?

Gilbert What a pity. And you all dressed up. Where did you meet her, anyway?

Mark At the squash club.

Gilbert I didn't know she played squash. I would have thought aerobics was enough to be going on with. But if she's out, how did you get in?

Mark The kitchen door was open.

Gilbert Was it? I shall have to speak to Mrs Capstick about that. She's always going out and leaving things. Anyone could wander in. And they *did*, didn't they? Well — *you* did.

Mark I wasn't expecting *you* to be here!

Gilbert No, I'm sure you weren't! You thought I was safely out of the way in Düsseldorf! Well, I *am* here and my wife's *not*, so there's no point in your hanging about. (*He tries to urge him on his way again*)

Mark Didn't you have the decency to leave when it didn't work out?

Gilbert (*puzzled*) Sorry?

Mark You needn't pretend! She told me all about it.

Gilbert At the squash club?

Mark The poor woman's terrified of you!

Gilbert Is she? I didn't know that.

Mark After the way you've treated her?!

Gilbert Don't be silly. She doesn't know about Düsseldorf.

Mark What?

Gilbert Never mind ...

Mark Perhaps you've just come back to collect your things? Is that it? And not a moment too soon! I expect you've left socks and shirts lying about all over the place. Toothbrush next to hers in the bathroom. It's obscene!

Gilbert (*at a loss to understand this extraordinary outburst*) Now look here, I think I've been very patient with you up to now, but I've had a tiring day and I've got something to see to upstairs, so I'd be glad if you'd get the hell out of my house.

Mark (*wildly*) *You*'re the one who should be going! You don't belong here anymore!

Gilbert (*calmly*) Don't be silly. You've just seen my photograph and I've shown you my latchkey, so on your bike!

Mark (*surprised*) How did you know?

Gilbert Sorry?

Mark That I came here on a motorbike.

Gilbert (*amused*) You didn't, did you? (*He chuckles*) On your bike wearing a dinner jacket? Did anybody see you?

Mark One or two people looked.

Gilbert Laughed a bit, I expect?

Mark No!

Gilbert I'm very surprised. Right — off you go, then! Don't hang about! I'll tell my wife you called and didn't get dinner. (*He pushes Mark towards the hall*)

Helga comes down the stairs. She is now rather scantily clad in a flimsy négligé and is carrying a glass of champagne

Helga Gilbert, how much longer are you going to keep me waiting?

Mark looks at her in surprise. Gilbert is frozen. A dreadful pause

Gilbert Haven't you finished upstairs *yet*?

Helga (*giggling*) Well, I'm not going to start on my own!

Gilbert (*turning to Mark; smiling innocently*) This is the cleaning lady.

Mark *Another* one?!

Gilbert What?

Mark There's been one of those here already.

Gilbert Has there? Well, it's a very big house.

Helga (*to Gilbert; angrily*) You have another lady?

Gilbert No, no!

Mark Yes, you have! I saw her driving away as I arrived. Going too fast for my liking.

Gilbert Oh, Mrs Capstick's very reckless behind the wheel.

Mark She doesn't *look* like a cleaning lady.

Gilbert Mrs Capstick? You should see her legs! All sticking out at the — (*he demonstrates on his own legs*)

Mark Not her! *This* one! Why is she dressed like that?

Gilbert Because she's cleaning the bedrooms, of course. She's the *upstairs* cleaning lady. Mrs Capstick just does the downstairs, so *she*'d be the one wearing an apron.

Mark And do you always give champagne to your cleaning ladies?

Gilbert Certainly. We know how to treat our staff in Little Bendon. We look after them, and they look after us. (*He joins Helga, proudly*)

Helga (*suddenly pointing at Mark*) Who *is* this man?

Gilbert I'm not quite sure. He says he's here to have dinner with my wife.

Helga (*alarmed*) She's not here, is she?

Gilbert No, of course she isn't!

Helga Come on, then, liebling ... (*she smiles at him and clings on to his arm, provocatively*)

Mark (*observing Helga*) She's very friendly for a cleaning lady.

Gilbert Well, I'm a great believer in domestic democracy.

Helga (*to Gilbert; quietly*) Why don't you get rid of him?

Gilbert He's just going.

Helga Good! I will be waiting for you ...

She smiles seductively and disappears upstairs

Gilbert (*looking at Mark and shrugging helplessly*) You see my problem,
don't you? I'll have to go and show her how to do it. (*He urges Mark
towards the hall*)

Mark I should think she *knows* how to do it!

Gilbert The cleaning! She's new here. Doesn't know where we keep the
dusters. Come on, then! Off you go!

*Gilbert propels Mark ahead of him, and they go into the hall. The front
door slams and then Gilbert returns*

Looking relieved and smiling, optimistically, he runs out up the stairs

*As he disappears, Jane comes in from the dining-room, talking as she
arrives*

Jane Mark, are you going to stay out here all — ? (*She stops, seeing no
sign of him*) Mark ... Mark ...? (*Puzzled, she goes across to look out into
the hall*)

*Behind her, the kitchen door bursts open and Mark almost falls into the
room, breathless*

(*Jumping a mile*) Aah! Mark — what *are* you doing?

Mark I ... I felt like a breath of air. So I ... I had a run around the garden.
(*He runs on the spot, briefly*)

Jane Whatever's the matter? You didn't find one, did you?

Mark Find one?

Jane A burglar! You were looking for a burglar!

Mark Oh — yes. Yes, I was, wasn't I ...?

Jane But you didn't?

Mark What?

Jane Find one!

Mark No. Not a *burglar* ...! (*He casts a quick, anxious look towards the
stairs*) We can't stay here!

Jane What?

Mark We've got to go!

Jane But the evening's only just beginning.

Mark No, it isn't! It's over!

Jane Over?

Mark Yes!

Jane You know, you really are bad for my morale. I arranged all this specially.

Mark I don't want your husband to find you here!

Jane He's not likely to do that. He's miles away.

Mark That's what *you* think ...!

Jane heads towards the kitchen

Where are you going?

Jane To get the champagne.

Mark I don't want champagne!

Jane Well, *I* do! (*She stomps off into the kitchen*)

Mark gives a quick, anxious look towards the stairs, and then runs out into the hall urgently

Jane returns, looking very puzzled. Then she is surprised to find that he has disappeared again

Mark ...? Mark — where the hell have you gone *now*?

Mark returns with his motorbike gear and dumps it on the sofa

What on earth are you doing?

Mark Getting dressed.

Jane Why?

Mark Because we're leaving! (*He starts getting dressed at high speed*)

Jane But we haven't got into the swing of it yet ...

Mark Well, we can't stay here!

Jane Somebody might ring up to see how we're getting on.

Mark (*puzzled*) What?

Jane I told you — the neighbours are very friendly in Little Bendon! (*Then, thoughtfully*) I could have sworn there was a bottle of champagne in the fridge ...

Mark (*busy dressing*) I think the cleaning lady took it.

Jane Oh, no. Mrs Capstick would never drink champagne. Mark, for heaven's sake! You should be taking your clothes *off*, not putting them *on* ...

Mark I've got to take you away from this house — *now*!

Jane There's plenty of time! And we've got the whole house to ourselves ...

Mark Oh no, we haven't ...!

Jane What?

Mark (*by now fully dressed in his motorbike gear*) We can't stay here! Come on!

Jane But it's getting foggy out there! And I haven't cleared away the dinner things.

Mark Never mind the dinner things! I'll get my bike started! (*He runs out into the kitchen*)

Jane But, Mark — !

The kitchen door shuts in her face

Oh, blast!

Gilbert comes running downstairs, having heard voices

Gilbert What the hell's going on down here?

He comes face-to-face with Jane, and they stare at each other for a moment, frozen like statues

Jane ...!

Jane Gilbert ...!

Gilbert Well, at least we know who we are.

Jane How long have you been here?

Gilbert Seven and a half years.

Jane Tonight! I thought you were going to Düsseldorf.

Gilbert So did I ...! Have you just arrived?

Jane Er ... yes.

Gilbert (*going to her*) I suppose *you* got in through the back door as well?

Jane Ah — yes — that's right — I did!

Gilbert I shall have words with Mrs Capstick in the morning. She must learn to lock up when she leaves. Still — lucky for you, eh? If *she* hadn't left the door open, *you'd* still have been outside! (*He laughs*)

Jane Yes ... (*she giggles nervously*)

Gilbert Don't tell me *you*'ve come to dinner, too?

Jane Er ... what?

Gilbert Well, you seem to be all dressed up.

Jane Oh — *this*? It's nothing! Just something I picked up from Oxfam.

Gilbert Did you happen to see some lunatic in a dinner jacket driving off on a motorbike?

Jane Er ... when?

Gilbert Just now!

Jane No ...

Gilbert I thought you might have seen him leaving as you were arriving.

Jane No! I didn't see anybody! Er ... what was he doing here?

Gilbert Refusing to look at my photographs.

Jane Is he a friend of yours?

Gilbert No, he is *not*!

Jane Well ... did he tell you why he came here?

Gilbert Yes, he certainly did!

Jane (*alarmed*) He *did*?!

Gilbert Oh, yes. He's taken a fancy to Shirley.

Jane To *Shirley*?

Gilbert Definitely gave that impression. You'll never believe this, but he came here to have dinner with her!

Jane (*assuming surprise*) He *didn't*!

Gilbert Yes. Only they'd messed up the arrangement, hadn't they, and fixed the wrong night?

Jane Really?

Gilbert Yes — Friday night is her aerobics night! I expect he thought he'd come here and try to seduce her while I was away in Germany. Dirty devil ...

Jane And why aren't you?

Gilbert Hmm?

Jane In Germany.

Gilbert Oh. Thick fog at the airport. So our flight was — er — *my*! — my flight was cancelled. (*He glances anxiously towards the stairs*) Anyway, what are *you* doing here? Don't say *you*'d forgotten about Shirley's aerobics class as well?

Jane Ah — yes! That's right! I had!

Gilbert Didn't you think to telephone? You don't usually pop in on the off-chance.

Jane Yes, I should have done ...
Gilbert So it's been a bit of a wasted journey for you, hasn't it?
Jane (*ruefully*) Yes, it certainly has ...!

Gilbert again looks towards the stairs nervously and moves nearer to Jane, anxious to be rid of her

Gilbert Right! Off you go, then!
Jane What?
Gilbert Well, there's no point in your hanging about here. Shirley won't
  be back for ages.

From upstairs comes Helga's plaintive cry:

Helga (*off*) Gilbert ... where are you ...?

Jane stares at Gilbert in surprise. He freezes, thinking desperately

Gilbert Will you excuse me a minute? I think I left the radio on upstairs.

He races out up the staircase at high speed. The moment he has gone, Jane runs out into the kitchen to make sure that Mark has gone. After a brief pause, she comes quickly back in and resumes her previous position before Gilbert comes running back down the stairs to rejoin her

  Yes. I had!
Jane What?
Gilbert Left it on upstairs.
Jane It didn't sound like the radio to me.
Gilbert Didn't it? Look, if I were you, I'd be on my way!
Jane You're very keen to get rid of me.
Gilbert Well, I'm rotten company tonight. No small talk at all. I've had
  a tiring day, you see, and all I want to do is get to bed.
Jane Does Shirley know you're here?
Gilbert What?
Jane Shirley. Your wife! Does she know you're not in Düsseldorf?
Gilbert Of course she doesn't!
Jane It'll be quite a surprise for her, then, when she gets back and finds
  you listening to the radio.

Gilbert (*looking anxiously at his watch*) She won't be back yet, will she? (*He realizes that he sounds guilty, and calms himself*) I mean — she's usually late after her aerobics. I think they pop into the pub for a pint. (*He looks out between the curtains*) I should get off, if I were you. The fog seems to be getting thicker.

Jane Oh, dear. Perhaps I'd better stay the night?

Gilbert (*loudly*) No!

Jane Whatever's the matter?

Gilbert It's ... it's not convenient. In fact, it's very *in*convenient. Anyway, I'm not married to you.

Jane No. But I'm a friend of the family.

Gilbert Are you?

Jane (*hurt*) Gilbert!

Gilbert Yes — yes, of course you are! But there's — there's no room!

Jane Don't be silly. You've got four bedrooms!

Gilbert Have I?

Jane And you can't be using them *all*.

Gilbert That's what *you* think ...!

Jane Are you feeling all right?

Gilbert Anyway, what about the neighbours? You know what they're like in Little Bendon. Always got their eyes pressed to the glass.

Jane They'd need to have in this fog.

Gilbert They'll know Shirley's out, and they'll think I've got a loose woman in here.

Jane (*suspiciously*) Perhaps you *have* ...?

Gilbert Of course I haven't! But that's what they'll think, having seen *you* arrive.

Jane Surely they know you'd never do a thing like that?

Gilbert Of course they do! But they ... they might wonder. You know what minds they've got in Little Bendon. And large trees from little acorns grow.

Jane What's that got to do with it?

The back door in the kitchen slams

Gilbert (*reacting to the noise*) What was that?

Jane Er ... what?

Gilbert There's somebody in the kitchen! (*He sets off towards the kitchen*)

Jane (*racing around to intercept him*) No! You mustn't go in there!
Gilbert What?
Jane It might be a burglar!
Gilbert If it is he's probably pinching Shirley's Moulinex mixer.
Jane Does it matter?
Gilbert Of course it matters! She's only just bought it. I don't think she's even used it yet. (*He tries to get past her*)
Jane But he might attack you!
Gilbert With a Moulinex mixer? Jane, will you please get out of the way!

The kitchen door opens and Mark comes in urgently, talking as he arrives

Mark (*his voice muffled by the helmet*) Are you coming or not? (*He stops as he sees Gilbert*)
Gilbert (*gazing at him; astonished*) Who the hell are *you*?

Mark removes his helmet

(*Smiling broadly*) Good Lord — it's old Dinner Jacket! You look like something from outer space. (*To Jane*) This is the one I was telling you about. (*To Mark*) I've just been telling Jane all about you!
Mark (*puzzled*) But she *knows* all about me.
Gilbert Does she?
Mark Of course she does!
Jane No, she doesn't!
Mark (*looking at her; astonished*) What?
Jane I don't know *anything* about you!
Mark (*to Jane*) We met at the squash club! (*To Gilbert*) We met at the squash club.
Jane No, we didn't!
Mark What ...?
Jane (*to Gilbert*) *I* don't know *him*, and *he* doesn't know *me*!
Gilbert That's what I thought ...
Mark (*to Jane*) Have you gone mad?
Gilbert (*to Mark; keen to be rid of him*) I didn't expect you to be still hanging about! I thought you'd be halfway home by now.
Mark (*aggressively*) I'm not going without her!

Gilbert Without who?

Mark Without Jane!

Gilbert Oh. Well, that's very thoughtful of you. It is a nasty night. Might be a good idea to go in convoy.

Mark I'm going to drive her!

Gilbert You make her sound like a flock of sheep.

Mark I'm going to drive her on my bike!

Gilbert (*amused*) You're not, are you? (*To Jane*) Do you fancy being perched on his pillion?

Jane No, I do *not*!

Gilbert I'm not surprised. (*To Mark*) You needn't bother. She's got her own car. So she can follow your tail-light.

Mark (*moving closer to Gilbert; intensely*) Do you understand what I'm saying?

Gilbert Er ... yes. I think so ...

Jane (*quietly*) I hope you don't ...!

Mark I'm not leaving Jane alone in this house with you!

Gilbert Quite right. That's just what *I* said. She can't stay here. What would the neighbours think?

Mark What sort of a man *are* you?

Gilbert Well, I'm not a bad sort of a chap, really. Once you get to know me. Perhaps a little impetuous, occasionally ...

Mark Now, look here —— !

Jane Do we have to discuss this *now*? (*She glares at Mark pointedly*) I thought you were going? I'll follow you in my car!

Mark (*persisting; to Gilbert*) Aren't you even going to do the decent thing?

Gilbert What's that?

Mark *You* go — and leave Jane to stay *here*!

Gilbert Oh, I don't think I could do that. Anyway, Jane's anxious to be on her way. Aren't you, Jane?

Jane Yes — (*quietly*) I am *now* ...!

Gilbert Right! That's settled! Off you go, then, and leave me to get on with it.

Jane Get on with what? Listening to the radio?

Gilbert Locking up! All that. Doors. Windows. I don't want any more people wandering in tonight.

Jane (*to Mark*) You go on! I'll catch you up. I'll just go upstairs and get my things.

Gilbert What things?

Jane My coat and bag.

Gilbert What on earth are your coat and bag doing upstairs? I thought you'd just arrived.

Mark (*to Gilbert; appalled*) You mean you don't even let her keep her things here?

Gilbert Well, Jane doesn't *usually* leave her things lying about upstairs.

Mark Oh, my God ...!

Jane I'll just pop up and get them. (*She goes towards the stairs*)

Gilbert panics and races around to intercept her

Gilbert No! You can't go up those stairs!

Jane (*astonished*) Why not?

Gilbert They're very steep. Much *too* steep. I keep meaning to have them altered. We really ought to put a sign at the bottom saying, "Danger — Steep Hill". If you go up and down these stairs you'll be far too tired to drive your car. *I'll* get your things. (*He starts to go*)

Mark Don't *you* mind the steep stairs, then?

Gilbert Oh, I've got used to them by now. After all, I have lived here for seven and a half years.

Mark looks puzzled by this

(*To Jane*) Where did you leave them?

Jane In your bedroom.

Gilbert Oh, my God ...!

Gilbert runs up the stairs at high speed and out to the bedrooms

Mark (*moving to Jane*) Why are you pretending you don't know me?

Jane Because I don't want Gilbert to know that we were here together!

Mark But I've already told him.

Jane He's taking it very calmly.

Mark (*suspiciously*) Yes, he is, isn't he? That's probably because of the new cleaning lady ...

Jane (*puzzled*) Cleaning lady?

Gilbert runs downstairs with Jane's coat and bag

Gilbert (*holding the bag aloft*) Is this it?
Jane Yes. That's the one.

Gilbert hastily helps Jane into her coat

Gilbert I can't think why you brought such a big bag. Do you always go
  to places all prepared to stay the night?
Jane Not always ...
Gilbert (*to Mark*) Have you left your telephone number?
Mark Sorry?
Gilbert (*abruptly*) For my wife! So she can telephone you about dinner!
Mark (*puzzled*) She doesn't *need* to telephone me, does she?
Gilbert Oh, all right. Please yourself. You gave me the impression that
  it was a matter of some importance!
Mark But I don't need to leave my number, do I? Not *now*!
Gilbert Don't you?
Mark Of course I don't!
Jane (*hastily*) Right! I'm ready! Off we go!
Mark (*to Gilbert*) But there's something I think *you* ought to know.
Gilbert *I* don't want your telephone number!
Mark As soon as *you're* out of the way — I want to get together with your
  wife!

He glares at Gilbert and goes into the kitchen

Gilbert You see what I mean? Do you think he's some sort of sex maniac?
Jane Oh, no, I don't think so ...!

Helga arrives and runs down the stairs

Helga Where have you gone? You keep on disappearing!

*She sees Jane. And Jane sees her. Both look surprised. Gilbert wishes he
were safely in Düsseldorf. Jane turns to Gilbert with a bright smile*

Jane The new cleaning lady, I presume?

Gilbert H-how did you guess?

Jane Female intuition.

Helga Oh, my God — you have come back early ...!

Jane Don't worry. I'm not his wife.

Helga (*relieved*) Oh, good ...!

Gilbert (*smiling; nervously*) I ... I haven't told Shirley about her, you see.

Jane No. I bet you haven't!

Gilbert I wanted it to be a surprise.

Jane Oh, I think it will be! She's not a bit like Mrs Capstick, is she?

Gilbert She's just finishing off upstairs and then I'm going to run her home.

Jane Well, I do hope she's going to put some clothes on first. You know what the neighbours are like in Little Bendon.

She smiles and goes into the kitchen, closing the door behind her

Gilbert *Now* see what you've done!

Helga I have not done *anything* yet ...

Gilbert She saw you! She's a friend of my wife and she saw you! And you know what women are like — they talk — and then it all comes out!

Helga You must not be angry with me ... (*She begins to cry*)

Gilbert Oh, I'm sorry, Helga — it's not your fault ——

Helga (*brightening at once*) Is there any more champagne?

Gilbert Don't say you've finished that lot already?

Helga What do you expect? You keep disappearing.

Gilbert Well, I had things to see to down here.

Mark's motorbike is heard driving off noisily

Helga But now they have gone ...

Gilbert Yes. I think so. (*He looks out between the curtains*) Yes. They've both gone. In all directions.

Helga (*approaching him; seductively*) So now we are alone ... at last ... just the two of us ...

Gilbert Yes ...

Helga And we have finished the champagne ...

Gilbert Well, *you* have ...

Helga So now — please — may we have "afters"?

Gilbert (*blankly*) What?

Helga After aperitif you promised me afters.

Gilbert Did I? (*He backs away nervously*)

Helga (*following him*) Yes, you did ...

Gilbert I ... I didn't think I'd made a firm commitment.

Helga You did! So now there is nothing to stop us, is there, liebling?

Gilbert Isn't there?

Helga Except for one thing.

Gilbert Oh, good. What thing is that?

Helga You still have got your clothes on.

Gilbert Have I? (*He looks*) Good Lord, so I have! I hadn't noticed.

Helga pushes him on to the sofa, kissing the sides of his face as she starts to remove his jacket. He mutters vague protestations as one side of his jacket comes off with the sleeve inside out. As Helga removes the second sleeve, Gilbert is putting his arm back into the first sleeve. In the end he is left with the jacket on back-to-front and inside-out, with a Lufthansa ticket sticking out of his inside pocket

Helga You don't usually take so long to get out of your clothes.

Gilbert No. I know. But it's different here!

Helga Why?

Gilbert I told you — this is my sitting-room! I'd feel embarrassed with my clothes off in my sitting-room.

Helga Would you feel happier if we went outside and sat in my car?

Gilbert (*staring at her; appalled*) Don't be ridiculous! It's foggy out there. I might get into the wrong gear.

Helga laughs delightedly and kisses him

(*Surfacing*) No! I mustn't ...!

Helga kisses him again

No! I won't ...!

She kisses him again

Oh, all right, but we'll have to be quick.

Helga grabs him enthusiastically

The front doorbell rings. Gilbert leaps away from her in a high state of alarm

There's somebody at the front door! There's somebody ringing the bell!
Helga (*calmly*) Are you expecting *more* visitors?
Gilbert Of course I'm not! (*He hastily takes off his jacket and puts it back on the right way round but still inside out*) It might be my wife!
Helga Why should your wife ring the doorbell? Hasn't she got her own key?
Gilbert She could have lost it!
Helga But why should she come home early?
Gilbert Maybe she slipped during her aerobics! Slipped and twisted her ankle! Oh, my God! She'll be out there now — lying on a stretcher!
Helga If she is lying on a stretcher she could not have *reached* the bell.
Gilbert There'll be people with her, won't there? Paramedics! *They'll* have rung the bell!

The doorbell rings again

There you are! They're getting impatient! It must be something serious! (*He grabs Helga's hand and drags her towards the kitchen*)
Helga Where are we going?
Gilbert If my wife's come home on a stretcher she mustn't find *you* here! (*He opens the kitchen door*)
Helga But why are you putting me in the kitchen? Why can't I wait for you upstairs?
Gilbert Because they'll carry her straight up there, won't they! And what's *she* going to say if she finds *you* in her bedroom?

Gilbert pushes her inside abruptly and closes the door. Then he runs out into the hall frantically

The moment he has gone, the curtains over the french windows are parted carefully and Roger looks in. He steps into the room, looking about. He is a large man in his forties, wearing an overcoat and carrying a small bunch of flowers

Gilbert returns from the hall, relieved

It's all right! There's nobody there! They must have — (*he stops, seeing Roger*) Who the hell are you?

Roger I rang the bell, but nobody answered.

Gilbert So you walked straight into my house?

Roger *Your* house? Ah! You must be Gilbert?

Gilbert You've heard of me?

Roger Oh, yes. But I didn't think you were going to be here.

Gilbert I *live* here!

Roger Yes, I know you *live* here. But I thought you were in Düsseldorf.

Gilbert That's what a lot of people thought. Well, I'm sorry to disappoint you, but my plane was grounded because of fog. (*He reacts*) Who told *you* I was going to be in Düsseldorf?

Roger Oh, I ... I heard it. From ... friends. That you would be.

Gilbert Do you and your friends spend a *lot* of time discussing my whereabouts?

Roger Oh. No — er ——

Gilbert Lucky for you I'm *not* in Düsseldorf.

Roger Oh?

Gilbert If I was in Düsseldorf you'd still be standing outside ringing the doorbell.

Roger Are you alone, then?

Gilbert None of your damn business.

Roger Excuse me, but (*he leans forward confidentially*) ... do you know that your jacket's on inside-out?

Gilbert stares at him stonily for a second, then looks down at his jacket. He reacts and hastily takes it off, turns it the right side out and puts it back on again

Gilbert I got dressed in the dark.

Roger (*surprised*) Really?

Gilbert Who are you, anyway?

Roger What?

Gilbert What are you doing here?

Roger What?

Gilbert Look — we're not going to get anywhere if you keep on saying 'what'.

Roger Shirley isn't here, then?

Gilbert What?

Roger Now *you're* doing it!

Gilbert What do *you* know about Shirley?

Roger I ... I know she's married to a man called Gilbert. Ah! (*He points at Gilbert, with a smile*)

Gilbert How do you know that?

Roger Jane told me. Jane's a friend of Shirley's.

Gilbert Yes. I know ...!

Roger Well ... that's how I know about Shirley.

Gilbert And how do you know about Jane? You're not another squash player, are you? You didn't arrive on a motorbike, by any chance? (*He chuckles*)

Roger Oh, no. I'm Jane's husband.

Gilbert Are you really? How do you do? (*He shakes Roger's hand*) I'm afraid you've just missed her.

Roger Missed Jane?

Gilbert Yes.

Roger (*surprised*) You mean she was *here*?

Gilbert Yes, it was a surprise to *me*, too!

Roger What was she doing here?

Gilbert I'm not quite sure ... (*He moves towards the staircase, looking out for any sign of Helga*)

Roger I thought she was going to her Old Girls' Reunion tonight. I can't think what she was doing turning up here ...

Gilbert Well, *you* did! *And* carrying a bunch of flowers!

Roger (*nervously*) What? Ah — yes — so I did ...

Gilbert Pity Shirley isn't here. *She* could have had them.

Roger (*alarmed*) No, no! They're not for her!

Gilbert What a pity. She doesn't often get flowers from strangers. Now, look, I really think ——

Roger (*profoundly*) I saw a man at the station.

Gilbert considers this

Gilbert Is that unusual?

Roger Selling flowers. Didn't have many left. A few carnations. Some gypsophilia. But they were hanging fire. Because of the fog, I suppose.

People don't bother with flowers when there's fog. He was selling them off cheap. And I never could resist a bargain. So I stopped the car. I gave him a couple of pounds, and he gave me these. He seemed very pleased. (*He stares bleakly at the flowers*) And they're quite nice, really, aren't they? Considering they've been standing about in the mist.

Gilbert (*bemused by this meandering dissertation*) Do you want to leave them here?

Roger (*pleased*) Oh? May I?

Gilbert Yes, of course. You don't want to go on driving around in the fog with a bunch of wilting flowers, do you?

Roger Perhaps I could put them in water? Is the kitchen through — ? (*He sets off towards the kitchen*)

Gilbert (*giving chase*) No!!

Roger What?

Gilbert There isn't any!

Roger No kitchen?

Gilbert No water! They've turned it off.

Roger Turned off the water?

Gilbert Because of the fog. They always seem to turn off the water when there's a fog.

Roger Why?

Gilbert Don't ask me! *I* don't make the rules. So you'll have to leave them here. I'll put them in water once we're reconnected. (*He takes the flowers and puts them down*)

Roger Oh. Right. Thank you ... (*he stands, waiting*)

Gilbert Well? What are you waiting for? You want me to give you two pounds?

Roger (*puzzled*) Sorry?

Gilbert Refund. For the flowers.

Roger Oh — no — please! My pleasure.

Gilbert Right! You'd better be on your way, then!

But at that moment Helga walks out of the kitchen

Helga Is it safe now to come out of the kitchen?

Gilbert and Roger stare at her, frozen for a moment

Gilbert She ... she was just getting me some Horlicks. I want to be sure of a good night.

Helga (*to Roger*) So it was *you* ringing the doorbell?

Roger I'm afraid so ...

Helga (*giggling*) Gilbert thought you might be his wife!

Roger (*embarrassed*) I do hope I'm not interrupting anything ...?

Helga } (*together*) { Yes! You are!
Gilbert } { No! You're not!

Gilbert (*going to her, urgently*) Isn't it time you got off home, Helga? (*To Roger*) She was just finishing off in the kitchen.

Roger Sorry?

Gilbert Didn't you hear about her from Shirley?

Roger Oh, I don't really know Shirley. Only *of* her.

Gilbert Well, if you *did* know her she'd have told you. (*He indicates Helga*) This is our new cleaning lady.

Roger (*puzzled*) Why is she dressed like that?

Gilbert Have *you* ever tried cleaning a kitchen?

Roger Well — yes, but ——

Gilbert It's very hot work. Far too hot to keep all your clothes on.

Roger And that's why she's — ? (*He indicates Helga's scanty négligé*)

Gilbert Exactly! But now she's finished she'll be putting them on again.

Helga No, I will *not* ...! (*She sits on the sofa, defiantly*)

Gilbert Of course you will! You can't go off to Düsseldorf dressed like that.

Roger (*puzzled*) Düsseldorf?

Gilbert She was just finishing off here, and then she was going to visit her mother.

Roger (*astonished*) In Düsseldorf?

Gilbert Yes.

Roger But you said it was too foggy to go to Düsseldorf, and that's why you were here and not there!

Gilbert Ah. Yes. I did, didn't I?

Roger So she can't go to see her mother, can she?

Gilbert Well ... no. Not now the fog's come down. But she *was*!

Roger (*smiling*) So if it hadn't been for the fog, you might have been on the plane *together*?

Helga (*starting to cry*) Oooooo ...!

Gilbert *Now* see what you've done! (*He goes to comfort Helga*) It's all right. There's nothing to cry about. You can see your mother *next* weekend. (*To Roger*) Very emotional, these German girls.

Roger I'll see if it's lifting.

Gilbert (*blankly*) What?

Roger The fog.

Gilbert Oh — yes.

Roger goes to look out of the french windows. Helga is using the excuse of Gilbert's comforting arms to snuggle up to him seductively

Gilbert Now, now! Easy, Helga ...!

Helga (*whispering*) What is he doing here?

Gilbert (*whispering also*) *I* don't know!

Roger It's getting thicker every minute.

Gilbert (*blankly*) What?

Roger The fog.

Gilbert Oh — yes.

Helga (*whispering*) Is that why he came here? Because of the fog?

Gilbert I'll ask him. (*To Roger*) Is that why you came here? Because of the fog?

Roger (*grateful for the suggestion*) Ah! Yes!

Gilbert What?

Roger (*wandering back to them*) There I was, you see? Driving along. Quite slowly as a matter of fact. About fifteen miles an hour, I should think. With my flowers.

Gilbert Oh, this was after you'd spent your two pounds?

Roger (*sitting cosily with them on the sofa*) Oh, yes. And the fog was (*he gestures*) — you know, closing in. Very difficult to see. That's why I was driving slowly. And then — I suddenly realized that I was quite near to where Jane told me *you* lived. You and ... er ...

Gilbert Shirley.

Roger Shirley. Right. So I thought — why not! Better safe than sorry. I'll stop at your house and ask if I can stay here until it (*he repeats the gesture*) — blows over.

Gilbert But why didn't you tell me that as soon as you arrived?

Roger (*blankly*) What?

Gilbert You never mentioned it before.

Roger Ah — well, I ... I suppose ... finding you here when I thought you were in ...

Helga Düsseldorf ...! (*She cries and clings to Gilbert*)

Roger And you with your jacket on inside-out, I suppose it quite put it out of my mind.

Gilbert So you want to stay here until it ... (*he copies Roger's gesture*)

Roger Blows over. Yes.

Helga That might not be until the morning!

Roger I hope that's not inconvenient.

Helga Yes — it is!

Gilbert Don't be silly! He can't drive home in the fog.

Roger (*getting up and moving away a little; smiling saucily*) And then *I* can be the chaperone.

Gilbert What?

Roger For you and the cleaning lady.

Gilbert (*moving to him; urgently*) She's not staying the night!

Helga (*jumping to her feet*) Yes, I am!

Gilbert No, you're not!

Roger She can hardly go home in the fog.

Gilbert Why not?

Helga (*smiling triumphantly*) If the fog is too thick for *him* to drive in, it is too thick for *me* to drive in, too.

Gilbert But my wife will soon be back from her aerobics!

Helga Not in this fog, liebling ...

Gilbert Ah. No ...

Roger And if *I* stay the night, too, you'll have nothing to worry about.

Gilbert Oh yes, I will! What will the neighbours think?

Roger Well, if *I'm* here, the neighbours won't be able to tell your wife that you were all alone in the house with the new cleaning lady. (*He smiles happily at this idea*)

Gilbert (*finding the idea quite pleasing*) No, they won't, will they? And after all, we do have plenty of rooms.

Roger Oh, good!

Helga (*to Gilbert, urgently*) Well, show him to his room *now*, then!

Gilbert (*embarrassed*) All right. There's no hurry!

Helga Yes, there is ...! (*She closes in on him sexily*)

Gilbert (*to Roger*) You're not in a hurry, are you?

Roger Well, I am feeling a little tired ...

Gilbert Yes. I suppose you would be after driving around in the fog looking for flowers.

Roger Could I ask you a favour?

Gilbert You already have.

Roger Next time you see my wife ... (*he hesitates*)

Gilbert Yes?

Roger Don't tell her that I stayed the night *here*.

Gilbert It's not a secret, is it?

Roger Oh, no! No, of course not! But ... Jane might wonder why I came here tonight when she was going to her Old Girls' Reunion.

Gilbert Would that matter?

Roger She might think it a little odd. With you supposed to be away in Düsseldorf. You know?

Gilbert (*grinning*) Ah — yes! I see what you mean.

Roger You know what women are like.

Gilbert I certainly do! (*He laughs*)

Roger So ... not a word to Jane, eh?

Gilbert You can rely on me.

Roger And then *I* won't tell Shirley about Helga.

Gilbert (*defensively*) There's nothing to tell! She's only the cleaning lady.

Roger But your wife might not believe that.

Gilbert Ah — yes — I see what you mean.

Roger You know what women are like.

Gilbert I certainly do! (*He laughs*) So ... not a word to Shirley, eh?

Roger You can rely on me.

Gilbert Right, then — I'll show you the way. (*As he leads Roger towards the stairs*) We've got four bedrooms — one to the left, three to the right. Mine's to the right. (*They go upstairs*)

Helga (*quietly*) So *he'd* better go to the left ...

Gilbert (*looking back*) What?

Helga (*pointedly*) Left!

Gilbert Ah — yes — you go to the left. Right? Er — left! The door facing you at the far end of the corridor. (*He points the way*)

Roger This is very kind.

Gilbert Not at all. What are friends for? Would you like an early call? Morning paper? Breakfast in bed?

Roger (*smiling; appreciating Gilbert's sense of humour*) Ah — yes — rather! (*He chuckles and starts to go*) Morning paper, eh? Two lightly-boiled eggs, a little brown toast, orange juice ... (*As he disappears to the left*) What a welcome ...!

Gilbert (*calling after him*) If you're cold in the night, you'll find a spare blanket in the wardrobe! (*He returns down the stairs to Helga*) I do hope I'm doing the right thing ...

Helga (*greeting him with a big smile*) Have you got any more champagne?

Gilbert What?

Helga Well — now there is no hurry, is there? We can have more aperitif ... and lots of afters! (*She kisses him and then goes towards the stairs*)

Gilbert But what about *him*?!

Helga *He's* not having any!

Gilbert No, no! (*Embarrassed*) But he'll ... he'll hear us.

Helga Don't be silly, liebling. He is to the left, and we are to the right. And we will be very quiet ...

She blows him a kiss and goes up the stairs

Gilbert That'll make a change ...

Helga turns

Helga What did you say?

Gilbert Nothing, darling! Just going to lock the front door.

Helga smiles and disappears to the bedrooms. Gilbert goes out into the hall

The kitchen door opens and Jane and Mark walk in, both a little weary after walking through the fog. Jane carries her bag

Gilbert returns from the hall and sees them. He looks alarmed

What the hell are *you* doing here?

Jane Coming back.

Gilbert You can't! It's far too late for coming back! I'm shut for the night!

Jane Gilbert — there's thick fog out there. It's far too thick to drive.

Mark So we had to abandon our vehicles and come back here. (*He puts his helmet down on the sofa*)

Gilbert I see. And what happened to "I'm not going to leave Jane alone in this house with you"?

Mark She won't *be* alone, will she? I'll be here. (*He starts to take off his leather jacket*)

Gilbert (*quietly*) You won't be the only one ...!

Mark I didn't come back here by choice, you know! There was no alternative. So now we'll have to spend the night here.

Gilbert You expect me to give you a bed for the night after you've thrown my photograph into the wastepaper basket?

Jane It was me who did that.

Gilbert (*going to her; surprised*) *You* did it as well? I'm very hurt. I thought that photograph was quite a good likeness. Shirley's very fond of it.

Mark Who's Shirley?

Gilbert (*to Jane; amused*) "Who's Shirley"!

Jane (*to Mark; quickly*) She's a friend of mine!

Gilbert She gets quite friendly with *me*, sometimes, too ...! (*He chuckles*)

Mark sits down to take off his boots. Jane, anxious to get off the subject of Shirley, takes her suitcase across to the stairs

Jane You don't *mind* if we stay here, do you, Gilbert?

Gilbert (*following her*) Yes, I do, as a matter of fact! I'd far rather you spent the night with one of the neighbours.

Jane (*astonished*) What?!

Gilbert They're very friendly here in Little Bendon. I'm sure someone would find you a bed for the night.

Jane Why can't we stay in *this* house?

Gilbert You wouldn't like it. It's far too crowded.

Jane You're the only person here.

Gilbert (*quietly*) That's what *you* think ...!

Jane What?

Gilbert We'll ring one of the neighbours — Mrs Ogshot — she's a very nice woman. (*To Mark*) You'll like Mrs Ogshot. She's got plenty of rooms.

Jane So have you!

Gilbert What?

Jane You've got four bedrooms.

Gilbert Have I?

Jane Yes!

Gilbert Well, some of them are occupied.

Jane Occupied?!

Gilbert I'm not sure where I'd put you both ...

Mark (*looking up from his boots*) I hope you're not expecting Jane to sleep in *your* room?

Gilbert No fear!

Mark Because I can tell you now — it's out of the question.

Gilbert It certainly is ...!

Jane (*suspiciously*) Gilbert, you seem very agitated. Did the cleaning lady get off all right?

Gilbert (*blankly*) What?

Jane Before the fog closed in.

Gilbert Ah. No. I'm ... I'm afraid not.

Jane You don't mean she's still here?

Gilbert Er ... yes. I'm afraid so. (*He smiles nervously*)

Jane Well — what a surprise!

Mark You've seen her, then?

Jane Yes, I certainly have!

Mark He says she's the upstairs cleaning lady! The one who does the bedrooms. (*He laughs and puts his boots with his jacket and helmet*)

Jane At this time of night? (*She looks at Gilbert, smiling wickedly*)

Gilbert You can't expect Mrs Capstick to do four bedrooms as well as all this! She's only here in the mornings. Anyway, she's no good on the stairs. Have you seen her legs? Dreadful!

Mark Not like this one! (*He starts to take off his over-trousers*)

Jane But couldn't Mrs Capstick come in the evening and do the bedrooms? Or perhaps you *prefer* someone younger?

Gilbert Look, it isn't what you're thinking!

Jane You don't know what I'm thinking.

Gilbert Oh, yes, I do!

Jane Where is she, then?

Gilbert Who?

Jane The cleaning lady with good legs who specialises in the bedrooms.

Gilbert Oh ... she's there *now*.

Jane Upstairs?

Gilbert Yes.

Jane Cleaning?

Gilbert Sleeping.

Jane Sleeping?!

Gilbert In bed. Sleeping in bed.

Jane Whose bed?

Gilbert My bed.

Jane *Your* bed?!

Gilbert Only polite. She's a guest.

Jane You said she was a cleaning lady.

Gilbert Yes, but if she's staying the night she becomes a guest. So I've put her in my room. Because that's the best room. And only the best room's good enough for a guest. I do know my manners. And, after all, she is a woman.

Mark She certainly is ...! (*He takes his motorbike gear out into the hall*)

Jane Couldn't she have slept elsewhere?

Gilbert Oh, no. That's where *I*'ll be.

Jane And she's sleeping now?

Gilbert Oh, yes. Dead to the world.

Jane (*with a suspicious smile*) She must have been exhausted ...

Gilbert What?

Mark (*returning*) So that's two people in two rooms.

Gilbert Is it?

Mark Well, you in one and her in one. That's two in two.

Gilbert So it is!

Mark And you've got four.

Gilbert Yes.

Mark So that leaves two. One for me, and one for her.

Gilbert Ah. Not quite.

Mark Not quite?

Gilbert No.

Jane Why not quite?

Gilbert The fourth room's a non-starter.

Jane Is it?

Gilbert Oh, yes. It's ... rather full at the moment.

Jane You don't mean there's somebody sleeping in there?

Gilbert No, no — of course not!

Jane Then how can it be full?

Gilbert Books.

Jane What?

Gilbert Stacks of books. Garden tools. My old toboggan. Box of Meccano. The Boy Scouts are collecting it all on Tuesday for their jumble sale. So until Wednesday I'm afraid there's only three.

Mark Three?

Gilbert Bedrooms. And four into three won't go.

Jane (*with apparent reluctance*) Then I suppose *I*'ll have to share a room with Mark.

Gilbert and Mark look surprised

Gilbert What?

Jane Well ... it is a crisis, isn't it? Fog does qualify as a crisis, doesn't it? And in a crisis we all have to make sacrifices and ... pull together.

Gilbert I don't think I could ask you to do that.

Jane But I don't mind, Gilbert.

Gilbert No. But somebody *else* might ...! Anyway, what would *Shirley* say?

Mark (*puzzled*) Shirley?

Jane We could sleep in *your* room. It's very large.

Gilbert The cleaning lady's in there!

Jane We could move her.

Gilbert She's asleep!

Jane Then she won't notice.

Gilbert You can't go carrying cleaning ladies in and out of bedrooms.

Jane Why not?

Gilbert Anyway, I couldn't let you share a room with *him*! That would be asking *too* much. Even in a crisis.

Mark Exactly! And I do have my principles.

Jane (*ruefully*) Yes, I know ...!

Mark (*glaring at Gilbert*) And no matter what I think of Gilbert, he'd still be in the house.

Gilbert (*quietly*) Yes. And he's not the only one ...! (*To Mark*) What's my being in the house got to do with it?

Mark I'm hardly going to share a room with a married woman when her husband's in the house!

Gilbert Ssh! You must keep your voice down!

Mark Why?

Gilbert He'll hear you!

Mark What?

Gilbert She'll hear you! The cleaning lady! (*To Jane*) It really would be better if you stayed down the road with Mrs Ogshot.

Jane We can't disturb Mrs Ogshot at this time of night. We'll have to stay here, and that's the end of it.

Gilbert (*quietly*) It probably *will* be ...!

Mark But we'll have to have one room each.

Gilbert (*reluctantly*) Oh, very well! You can have the other two rooms to the right.

Jane What about you?

Gilbert Never mind about me!

Jane But the cleaning lady with good legs is in your room.

Gilbert I know that!

Jane So where will *you* be sleeping, Gilbert? Or shouldn't I ask?

Gilbert I'll ... I'll sleep down here. On the sofa. I've done it before. I'll be all right. Don't you worry about me.

Mark I don't mind sleeping down here.

Gilbert No, no! Really! It'll be my pleasure. Well, not my pleasure, but I'll be quite all right down here. On my own. Off you go, then! Top of the stairs — turn right. My room's the first, you two can have the second and third. And don't make a noise on the landing!

Jane Why not?

Gilbert Well, you don't want to disturb the cleaning lady, do you?

Jane (*fed up*) Oh, come on, then, Mark. I'll show you the way. (*She picks up her bag*)

Jane and Mark start to go upstairs

Gilbert Hope you have a good night.

Jane (*grumbling*) We'll have a good night's *sleep*, that's for sure ...

Jane and Mark disappear

Gilbert smiles optimistically, gets a travelling rug from the chest and arranges it on the sofa. Then he runs across and switches off the main lights, leaving only the lamp on the table beside the sofa. He takes off his shoes and tiptoes up the stairs

Jane reappears on the landing

Gilbert!

Gilbert Aaaaah!

Gilbert almost falls back to the foot of the stairs, rushes back to the sofa and rearranges the rug elaborately

I thought you'd gone to bed!

Jane (*coming downstairs*) I suddenly thought I'd better telephone Roger. Let him know that I won't be home tonight.

Gilbert You needn't bother to do that ...! (*He laughs*)

Jane Why not?

Gilbert He's ... he's not there!

Jane He was when I left.

Gilbert Well, he's not now!

Jane How do you know?

Gilbert What?

Jane How do you know he's not there?

Gilbert He ... he telephoned.

Jane (*surprised*) Telephoned *here*?

Gilbert Yes — *I* was a bit surprised, too. I didn't think he'd know this number ...

Jane What did he want?

Gilbert You, of course!

Jane (*alarmed*) You didn't tell him I was here?

Gilbert Well, you weren't, were you? Not then. He must have rung here on the off-chance.

Jane Did he leave a message?

Gilbert Ah — yes! He ... he said he'd got caught in the fog.

Jane The same as us! (*She starts to go back upstairs*)

Gilbert Yes! Wasn't that a coincidence? So he's ... he's staying the night ... somewhere.

Jane Oh, good! That's all right, then, isn't it? I don't have to worry.

She goes contentedly to her bedroom

Gilbert (*grinning*) No. Not until the morning ...! (*He waits for a moment to give her time to get into her room, then tiptoes up the stairs again*)

The telephone rings. Gilbert stops at the top of the stairs and turns to glare at it. Wearily, he sets off down the stairs again to answer it. The telephone rings—once, twice, three times, four times—and stops abruptly, just as he reaches it. He sighs, and then goes back and yet again starts to tiptoe up the stairs in his socks, smiling hopefully

Jane reappears in a rush and looks over the bannisters

Jane Gilbert!
Gilbert Aaah!

Gilbert again almost falls as he hastily escapes to the bottom of the stairs

Jane Was that the telephone?
Gilbert Yes!
Jane (*fearfully*) You didn't answer it, did you?
Gilbert No! They rang off before I got there!
Jane (*smiling happily*) Oh, that's all right, then!

Jane disappears back to the bedrooms

Now completely fed up, Gilbert abandons his wicked intentions and returns, wearily, to the sofa. He lies down, wraps the rug around himself despondently and switches off the lamp

CURTAIN

ACT II

The same. The following morning

The curtains are still drawn, but the sun is peeping through here and there. The travelling rug has been removed from the sofa

The front door slams, and Shirley comes in from the hall. She puts down her handbag and draws back the curtains. The fog has cleared and the sun floods in

Helga, wearing her delightfully flimsy négligé, runs down the stairs

Shirley watches in surprise as she approaches. Helga stops, seeing Shirley, and smiles cheerfully

Helga Guten Morgen!
Shirley Oh — yes. It is.
Helga The fog has all gone.
Shirley Yes ...

Helga goes into the kitchen

Shirley stands still, wondering who the hell Helga is

Helga pops her head out from the kitchen

Helga Would you like some coffee?
Shirley Oh ... er ... no, thanks. I'll have some later.
Helga When you have done a bit of the housework?
Shirley Well ... yes.
Helga All right!

Helga disappears back into the kitchen

Shirley sets off towards the stairs, then notices Gilbert's photograph is missing. She hesitates and bends down to peer into the wastepaper basket. She takes out the framed photograph of Gilbert, looks puzzled, dusts it off with her sleeve and puts it back in its usual position

Gilbert runs down the stairs urgently. He is wearing casual clothes. He stops as he faces an extremely surprised Shirley

Shirley Gilbert! What the hell are *you* doing here?

Gilbert W-what?

Shirley You're supposed to be in Düsseldorf!

Gilbert I was held up by the fog.

Shirley So was I.

Gilbert Ah! So that's why you didn't come home last night?

Shirley Yes ...

Gilbert Where did you stay, then?

Shirley When?

Gilbert Last night!

Shirley (*moving away*) Oh ... at Caroline's.

Gilbert Caroline Taylor's?

Shirley Yes. You remember Caroline?

Gilbert *I* came back here.

Shirley (*alarmed*) You didn't!

Gilbert I got back before it was too thick.

Shirley Back *here*?

Gilbert Yes.

Shirley (*hopefully*) You mean — this morning?

Gilbert No, no — last night.

Shirley (*appalled*) Last night?!

Gilbert Yes!

Shirley (*furiously*) Couldn't you have stayed at the airport hotel? Then you'd have been all ready for the off this morning. There must have been an early flight. You could have got on that. You'd have been in Düsseldorf by now. There was no point in coming back here!

Gilbert considers this tirade for a moment

Gilbert I'm glad you're pleased to see me. Pity *you* weren't here last night.

Shirley Why? What happened?

Gilbert You could have introduced me to this chap!

Shirley W ... what chap?

Gilbert The chap who was here last night!

Shirley I ... I didn't know there *was* a chap here last night.

Gilbert There! I told him you must have forgotten! (*He glares at her*) Bit of a wasted journey for him, wasn't it?

Shirley W-was it?

Gilbert Anyway ... he told me all about you and him!

Shirley *Me* and him?

Gilbert Yes. After he threw my photograph into the wastepaper basket.

Shirley I wondered how that got there ...

Gilbert Taken a fancy to you, hasn't he?

Shirley Not to *me*, no ...!

Gilbert (*chuckling*) You should have seen him! All dressed up in a dinner jacket!

Shirley (*amused*) *What*?

Gilbert Obviously wanted to make an impression on you. And you know what? Had the cheek to say that once I'm out of the way he wants to get together with you!

Shirley I ... I'm not quite sure who you're talking about ...

Gilbert Don't tell me you've got *dozens* of men in dinner jackets who want to get together with you? His name's Mark! You met him at the squash club!

Shirley I ... I don't know who you mean. W ... what did he look like?

Gilbert He'll be down in a minute. You can see for yourself.

Shirley (*appalled*) You mean he's still here?

Gilbert Of course he's still here! They're *all* still here! You were very popular last night.

Shirley W-was I?

Gilbert Oh, yes. *He* came to see you, and *she* came to see you.

Shirley She?

Gilbert Your friend Jane!

Shirley (*overdoing it a bit*) Jane came *here*?

Gilbert Yes. Don't you women ever listen to each other? She'd forgotten all about it being your aerobics night.

Helga comes out of the kitchen with a mug of coffee and a plate of buttered toast

Gilbert freezes in alarm

Helga I got myself some coffee and a little toast. (*She crosses to the stairs, smiling happily at Gilbert*) I am going to have it upstairs in your bed. (*She stops and looks back at Shirley*) I have finished in the kitchen if you want to start cleaning in there, Mrs Capstick.

Helga disappears upstairs

A pause. Gilbert suffers. So does Shirley

Shirley I'm very hurt ...
Gilbert I — I can explain — !
Shirley Do I *really* look like Mrs Capstick?
Gilbert (*with a nervous laugh*) No — of course not, darling! How can she possibly know what Mrs Capstick looks like?
Shirley Anyway, Mrs Capstick doesn't come on a Saturday.
Gilbert Well, *she* doesn't know that, does she?
Shirley (*with a touch of ice*) Is she a friend of yours?
Gilbert Er ... sorry?
Shirley Well, she seems to be making herself so at home I assume she must know somebody who lives here.
Gilbert No, no! She's ... foreign, that's all. Not so reserved as we English. More friendly ... outgoing — you know?
Shirley You mean she's a tart?
Gilbert No!
Shirley All right, then, Gilbert — who is she and what the hell is she doing in our bedroom?
Gilbert She's ... she's been staying the night.
Shirley Yes, I gathered that! But why?
Gilbert Because I asked her to.
Shirley I *bet* you did!
Gilbert No, no — it wasn't like that — !
Shirley Well, whoever she is, Gilbert, I don't think she should be eating toast in bed. She'll get crumbs under the duvet.
Gilbert Yes — right. I'll go and tell her. (*He starts to go, very quickly*)
Shirley What's her name?
Gilbert (*putting the brakes on*) What?

Shirley I presume she does have a name?

Gilbert Oh, yes — er — Helga. Helga something-or-other.

Shirley I didn't know we knew a Helga something-or-other ...

Gilbert No, we don't! Didn't!

Shirley But we do now? Well, *you* do, anyway. I suppose you must meet lots of Helgas in Düsseldorf?

Gilbert No! Never! None!

Shirley So who is she?

Gilbert She's ... she's the new cleaning lady.

Shirley I didn't know Mrs Capstick was leaving.

Gilbert Well — you know what Mrs Capstick's like upstairs! Takes her all her time to do the downstairs these days. And when she tries to go upstairs you'd think she was climbing Everest. Helga will be much better upstairs.

Shirley Yes, I'm sure she will ...! But how did ... Helga come to be here last night?

Gilbert (*expansively*) Ah — well — she was caught in the fog, wasn't she?

Shirley Just like us?

Gilbert Exactly! And she happened to be passing this house. So she ... she rang the doorbell ——

Shirley And you dragged her in?

Gilbert And I dragged her — No! I didn't *drag* her in! She ... she walked in. I could hardly leave her outside on a night like that, could I? She'd have got cold.

Shirley Why? Didn't she have a barrel of brandy round her neck?

Gilbert (*blankly*) What?

Shirley So after you'd let her in — what happened?

Gilbert Oh ... nothing much.

Shirley I *am* surprised ...

Gilbert We ... we got talking. You know how you get talking. Well, we did. Had quite an interesting conversation, as a matter of fact ...

Shirley And she said, "My name's Helga and I'm looking for a job as an upstairs cleaning lady"?

Gilbert No, no! (*With a nervous laugh*) No, she ... she didn't blurt it out like that! It just sort of ... came out in the conversation.

Shirley And *you* said, "What a coincidence — we're about to give Mrs Capstick the chop and can you start upstairs now?"

Gilbert sees the hopelessness of his case, and shakes his head solemnly

Gilbert It was a mistake ...
Shirley You bet your sweet life it was a mistake!
Gilbert An error of judgement.
Shirley Definitely.
Gilbert I'm too kind, you see. Kind and gullible.
Shirley And sex-mad.
Gilbert I'll get rid of her. I'll tell her we're going to give Mrs Capstick another chance to master the stairs. (*He starts to go*)
Shirley And check the duvet!
Gilbert What?
Shirley For crumbs.
Gilbert Ah — yes — right. (*Chattily*) Did you have a good aerobics class?

He sees her stern look

Well, we'll talk about that later ... (*He stumbles out up the stairs*)

The front door slams, and Jane comes in from the hall. She is wearing an overcoat over casual day clothes

Shirley looks surprised and goes to her, urgently

Shirley I thought you'd gone! Your car wasn't outside.
Jane I've just been to fetch it.
Shirley Sorry?
Jane I left it down the road last night.
Shirley What on earth were you doing out there?
Jane Gilbert turned up!
Shirley Yes, I know! I've just seen him!
Jane So Mark and I were trying to go, but the fog was so thick we had to come back.
Shirley (*after a nervous glance towards the stairs*) I never dreamt that he'd turn up here! I thought he was safely out of the way in Düsseldorf. Must have been a nasty surprise for you.
Jane Yes, it was!
Shirley *I* thought everything was going according to plan. I telephoned and hung on for four rings as we arranged ——

Jane Yes — I heard it!

Shirley And as there was no reply I assumed the best and stayed the night with a friend.

Jane (*miserably*) Well, it *didn't* go according to plan ...

Shirley No. But at least Gilbert didn't catch you and Mark ...

Jane No. Chance would have been a fine thing! Mark seemed more concerned with morals than with me.

Shirley Even after the champagne?

Jane *He* didn't *want* any, and *I* didn't *get* any. It had disappeared.

Shirley What?

Jane All he was after was a can of lager. (*She takes off her coat*)

Shirley So what happened?

Jane Nothing. He locked his bedroom door.

Shirley Ah! You tried it, then?

Jane Only very tentatively. (*Fed up*) I *knew* this wasn't a good idea. I'm no good at this sort of thing. I'll never do it again.

She goes into the hall to hang up her coat, and then returns

Shirley It must have been a full house, then, with you and Mark, and Gilbert and the cleaning lady.

Jane Oh, you've met her?

Shirley (*grimly*) Yes, I've met her all right! And you know whose bed *she* was sleeping in? Mine and Gilbert's!

Jane But Gilbert wasn't in it!

Shirley He'd better not have been!

Jane No. He slept down here on the sofa.

Shirley You expect me to believe that? He didn't need to sleep on the sofa, anyway. We've got four bedrooms. He could have slept in the other one.

Jane He said it was full.

Shirley Full of what?

Jane Things he'd collected for the Boy Scouts' jumble sale.

Shirley The Boy Scouts' jumble sale was last week!

Jane He must have forgotten.

Shirley Gilbert's never collected for the Boy Scouts in his life!

Jane Anyway, there is *one* good thing.

Shirley (*doubtfully*) Is there?

Jane Yes! Gilbert doesn't know that Mark came here to meet *me*.

Shirley No! He thinks Mark came here to meet *me*!

Mark comes downstairs. He is wearing a short dressing-gown of Gilbert's over his shirt and pants

Mark (*singing*)   "Oh, what a beautiful morning
                                    Oh, what a beautiful day ———"
The fog's cleared completely. I had a wonderful night. Slept like a log!
Jane (*quietly*) Yes, you *would* ...!
Shirley (*aside, to Jane*) No wonder he didn't answer the door ...
Mark (*seeing Shirley*) Oh — sorry! I didn't know you had a visitor. (*He tries to make the most of the dressing-gown for modesty's sake*) Have you just popped in for coffee?
Shirley (*puzzled*) Sorry, I — ?
Mark Jane told me how friendly the neighbours are in Little Bendon. I'm Mark. I'm a friend of Jane's. (*He holds out his hand, but has to hastily clutch his dressing-gown to him*) Sorry ...
Jane Do forgive me! I've forgotten my manners in all the excitement. This is Shirley.
Mark Ah! So you're Shirley? They were talking about you last night.
Shirley I *am* flattered.
Mark You live quite near, do you?
Shirley Well, I ———
Jane (*quickly*) Yes, she does! Just down the road.
Shirley Ah — yes! I often pop in to see Jane. In fact, I'm in here so often I sometimes feel that this is *my* house!

Shirley and Jane laugh

Mark I came to see Jane.
Shirley Did you really? (*To Jane*) Why didn't you tell me?
Mark So it was a bit of surprise when Gilbert turned up.
Shirley Yes, I bet it was ...!
Mark He was supposed to be in Düsseldorf.
Shirley Yes, I know ...!
Mark I'm surprised he had the nerve to show his face! Still, he won't be living here much longer ...
Shirley (*without thinking*) Really? He's never said anything to *me* about moving ...
Jane (*glaring at Shirley*) Well, he's hardly likely to go blurting it out to the *neighbours*, is he?

Shirley (*remembering*) Ah — no — of course not!
Mark I didn't want Jane to stay in the same house as that man ...
Shirley Which man is that?
Mark Gilbert!
Shirley Oh — him! No, I should think not!
Mark But with the fog coming down we couldn't see to drive.
Shirley Well, never mind. Next time Gilbert's out of the way perhaps
   you'd like to try again? You can borrow my house anytime!

Jane glares at her

Mark *Your* house?
Shirley (*hastily*) Ah — yes — it's just a few doors down the road.

Mark looks puzzled by this offer

   Gilbert runs downstairs urgently. He stops when he sees them

Mark glares at him belligerently — and so does Shirley

   Well? Isn't she going?
Gilbert (*distracted*) Who?
Shirley The "cleaning lady"!
Gilbert She refuses to put her clothes on.
Shirley I bet she took them off quick enough!
Gilbert She says she can't eat toast and get dressed both at the same time.
Mark You're still here, then?
Gilbert (*looking at him blankly, surprised by his vehemence*) Sorry?
Mark You! Still here!
Gilbert (*reasonably*) Well, I haven't had my breakfast yet, have I?
Mark I'm surprised you've got the nerve to stay for breakfast! If I was
   in your position I'd have driven off the minute the fog had lifted.
Gilbert I think that's rather rude. After all, I did give you a bed for the
   night. I'm very surprised my wife even *considered* having dinner with
   you. Even if you *were* wearing a dinner jacket.
Mark At least I know how to treat a lady!
Gilbert Oh? And how is that?
Mark With respect!

Jane (*quietly; to Shirley*) Too *much* respect ...!

Jane and Shirley giggle together

Gilbert (*going to her; belligerently*) Had a word with him, have you, Shirley?
Shirley Sorry?
Gilbert About the cock-up over dinner last night.
Shirley Er — no — not yet ...

Shirley and Jane exchange a look

Mark What's it got to do with *her*?
Gilbert Oh, come on! It's too late now to start pretending. You made your position perfectly clear last night!
Mark I don't think we want to discuss my position in front of the neighbours, do we?
Gilbert (*with a puzzled smile*) Well, I wasn't thinking of continuing our conversation out in the street!
Mark I'm sorry, Shirley. Nothing personal, of course.
Gilbert Nothing personal? I think it's *very* personal! You come creeping in here in a dinner jacket on a foggy Friday night to have a secret dinner with my wife when you think I'm safely out of the way in Düsseldorf and you say it isn't personal?
Shirley Gilbert, I really don't think we ought to talk about this *now* ...
Gilbert Ah — no — of course not. (*He turns to Jane*) I'm sorry, Jane. This must all be very embarrassing for *you*.
Mark I would have thought it was more embarrassing for Shirley!
Gilbert (*glaring at him*) Well, you should have thought of that before, shouldn't you?
Mark I *said* we shouldn't discuss it in front of the neighbours!
Jane Oh, don't worry about her! She's very broad-minded.
Mark (*puzzled*) What?
Gilbert I just can't think how you came to make a date for dinner on a Friday night when Shirley knew she was going to her aerobics class ...
Mark (*looking even more bewildered*) What does it matter what night Shirley was going to her aerobics class?

Jane and Shirley look at each other in panic

Jane ⎱ (*together*) Mark! You must be dying for breakfast!
Shirley ⎰

Mark Oh — well — perhaps a cup of coffee ...?

Jane (*going to Mark; enthusiastically*) Scrambled eggs! Sausages!
Tomatoes! Anything! Come with me!

She leads him towards the kitchen. He looks back coldly at Gilbert

Mark Is it all right if I go into the kitchen with your wife?

Gilbert (*smiling*) Oh, I think *Jane* can manage a little scrambled egg! (*He
laughs*)

*Mark looks puzzled. Jane looks alarmed and drags him into the kitchen,
closing the door after them abruptly*

(*Smiling bleakly*) I think he's taken a bit of a dislike to me.

Shirley (*coldly*) He's not the only one ...!

Gilbert (*ignoring this*) I even offered to show him that photograph of me
on a camel in front of the pyramids.

Shirley The one with the big banana?

Gilbert Yes.

Shirley Oh, darling, that's a *lovely* picture!

Gilbert (*sulking a little*) He wasn't even interested. There's no pleasing
some people ... Mind you, I suppose it's not surprising. Under the
circumstances.

Shirley What circumstances?

Gilbert You and him, of course!

Shirley Gilbert, I can explain about that ——

Gilbert You needn't bother! *I* don't want to hear the sordid details. (*He
suffers suitably*) I'm ... I'm just a bit hurt, that's all. I didn't think you'd
be inviting another man in for dinner while I was slaving away in
Düsseldorf ... (*He sinks, suffering, into the armchair*)

Shirley It wasn't what you think — !

Gilbert I don't treat you badly, do I?

Shirley What?

Gilbert On the whole?

Shirley Not usually, no. Why?

Gilbert Mark said you were terrified of me.

Shirley (*smiling; warmly*) Of course I'm not, darling ...

Gilbert Oh, good! That's all right, then.

Shirley Are *you* terrified of *me*?

Gilbert (*smiling; warmly*) Of course I'm not, darling ...

Shirley Well, you *should* be!

Gilbert Why?

Shirley You don't expect me to believe that she just appeared out of the fog, do you?

Gilbert (*blankly*) Who?

Shirley Helga!

Gilbert (*who hoped she had forgotten*) Good Lord! I'd forgotten all about her ...

Shirley *I* hadn't!

Gilbert (*heavily pathetic*) Well, I'm wounded. That's all. Deeply wounded ... How could you invite him to dinner?

Shirley (*blankly*) Who?

Gilbert Mark!

Shirley I'm sure she must have finished by now!

Gilbert (*blankly*) Who?

Shirley Helga!

Gilbert (*suffering again*) Can't you see that I'm suffering?

Shirley Good! So am I! She can't still be eating toast, surely? She's had time to finish the entire loaf!

Gilbert (*getting up with a weary sigh*) Oh, very well! I'll go and see!

Gilbert disappears upstairs

Shirley goes towards the kitchen. She notices Roger's small bunch of flowers that are still on the sofa table. Puzzled, she picks them up and looks at them, shrugs, and takes them into the kitchen

Gilbert returns furtively, tiptoes down the stairs and out into the hall. After a moment he returns carrying his raincoat. He crosses towards the stairs

Shirley returns from the kitchen, putting Roger's flowers into a vase

Gilbert panics, rolls the raincoat up into a ball and pushes it up under his sweater, which gives him the appearance of having a large stomach. Shirley sees him

He smiles nervously, tries to hide the large stomach from her, and hastens up the stairs. Puzzled, Shirley puts down the vase of flowers and goes back into the kitchen, closing the door behind her

Roger appears at the top of the stairs, coming from his bedroom. He is in his bare feet and is putting his overcoat on over his vest and pants. He comes downstairs, totally lacking in confidence in the strange house and clutching his coat to him modestly. He looks about, uncertain of where to go, thinking he is alone in the house with Gilbert and the cleaning lady with good legs

Mark comes out of the kitchen carrying a small tray

He heads for the dining-room but stops when he comes face-to-face with Roger. They contemplate each other for some time in bewildered silence. Roger bends his knees, trying to make his overcoat cover his bare legs. Mark holds the tray in front of his nether regions

Mark (*finally*) I'm just going to collect the dirty dinner plates.
Roger Oh.
Mark From last night. Fresh salmon!
Roger Really? (*He nods his approval*) Very nice ...

Mark continues towards the dining-room, then returns to Roger

Mark Is ... is anybody seeing to you?
Roger Sorry?
Mark I mean ... they do know you're here?
Roger Oh, yes. Well ... *he* does.
Mark Who?
Roger Gilbert.
Mark You know Gilbert?
Roger We have met, yes. I didn't think he was going to be here ...
Mark Neither did I! (*Confidentially*) I can't stand him.
Roger Oh, he seemed pleasant enough. Even offered me breakfast in bed.
Mark (*staring at him in surprise*) You mean you've been here all night?
Roger Well, you don't think I arrived without my trousers on, do you? (*He laughs, looking down at his bare legs*) Don't suppose *you* came looking like *that*, either!

Mark Oh, no. I was wearing a dinner jacket.

Roger Are they very formal in Little Bendon, then?

Mark I came here for dinner.

Roger Ah.

Pause. Both are deeply puzzled

I didn't get any.

Mark Dinner?

Roger Breakfast. In bed.

Mark Oh. Perhaps you'd like a cup of coffee.

Roger Is there any water?

Mark Sorry?

Roger There wasn't any water last night.

Mark Really?

Roger No. They turned it off because of the fog.

Mark Why did they do that?

Roger I'm not sure. I think it must be a local by-law ...

Mark Well, it's on all right this morning. There's plenty for coffee.

Roger (*going to look at the vase of flowers*) Ah, yes! I see there's some here in this vase.

Mark I don't think we'll be using that ...!

Roger (*peering closely at the flowers*) My flowers are recovering, anyway. They were looking a little limp last night.

Mark You brought flowers?

Roger Oh, yes.

Mark Do you usually bring flowers for Gilbert?

Roger No, no! They weren't for Gilbert. There was this old man, you see? At the station. Selling flowers in the middle of the fog. Well ... trying to. I told Gilbert, people don't bother with flowers when there's a fog. So I got a bit of a bargain. Why did you come to have dinner with Gilbert if you didn't think he was going to *be* here?

Mark No, no! I came to have dinner with his wife!

Roger (*astonished*) *Gilbert's* wife?

Mark Yes. He was supposed to be in ——

Roger Düsseldorf.

Mark Yes.

Roger But the fog came down?

Mark Yes. So the three of us stayed the night here.

Roger I see ... I didn't know about *that* ...!

Pause

Mark (*puzzled*) Where were *you* sleeping, then? I didn't think there was a spare room. (*A sudden amusing thought*) You weren't in with the cleaning lady, were you?

Roger The one with the legs?

Mark Ah! You've seen them?

Roger Oh, yes.

Mark Well ...? (*He smiles hopefully*)

Roger Oh, *no*! Top of the stairs. Turn left.

Mark Left?

Roger Yes.

Mark (*realizing*) Ah! You came to collect the jumble?

Roger Sorry?

Mark Books, garden tools, old toboggan, box of Meccano — that sort of thing?

Roger What are you talking about?

Mark For the Boy Scouts! (*He gives a Boy Scout salute*)

Roger (*irritably*) Do I *look* like a Boy Scout? There was no jumble in *my* room!

Mark Don't say they came in and collected it when we were all asleep!

Roger (*thinking Mark is mad*) Perhaps I *will* have a cup of coffee ...

Mark Yes — right! The kitchen's through there. I'll just collect the dirty dishes. Won't be a minute!

He disappears gratefully into the dining-room

Roger remains rooted to the spot, totally bemused, looking after Mark

Shirley comes out of the kitchen with a mug of coffee, closing the door behind her. She sees Roger and reacts with alarm

Shirley Roger ...!

Roger Shirley ...!

Shirley What are *you* doing here?

Roger (*smiling cheerfully*) Just getting up. Isn't it a lovely morning?

Shirley (*appalled*) You ... you mean you've been here all night?

Roger Oh, yes. I got caught in the fog, you see.

Shirley But why are you here?

Roger I was looking for *you* ... (*He smiles at her warmly*)

*Shirley casts an anxious look towards the kitchen, then goes closer to him
and speaks in hushed but affectionate tones*

Shirley Oh, darling — Friday's night's my aerobics night! I thought I'd
told you that?

Roger I must have forgotten.

Shirley Whatever did he say?

Roger Who?

Shirley Gilbert! You must have seen Gilbert!

Roger Oh — yes. And it was a bit of a surprise, I can tell you. I thought
he was in Düsseldorf.

Shirley Well — did he say anything?

Roger Yes. He offered me a bed for the night. You know — on account
of the fog.

Shirley Did you tell him who you were?

Roger (*laughing*) Of course I did!

Shirley And did he ask what you were doing here?

Roger No. I think he had other things on his mind. (*He leans forward
confidentially*) He had his jacket on inside out. (*He chuckles at the
memory*)

Shirley But, Roger — why did you come here?

Roger To bring you some flowers.

Shirley (*warmly*) Oh, darling ... (*she gives a quick, furtive look around
and then kisses him on the cheek — a hasty peck*)

Roger They're over here. (*He goes to the vase of flowers*)

Shirley I wondered where they came from ...

Roger They were a bit limp last night, but they're beginning to perk up
now. Lucky they turned the water back on.

Shirley (*puzzled*) What?

Roger After the fog.

*Shirley casts another anxious look towards the kitchen, and then leads him
away a little, out of earshot*

Shirley Roger ... it was very sweet of you to buy me flowers ...

Roger Oh, they only cost two pounds.

Shirley But you shouldn't bring me flowers *here* — this is where my husband lives!

Roger Well, there was this man, you see? At the station. Selling flowers. Well ... trying to. I told Gilbert, people don't bother with flowers when there's a fog ——

Shirley Roger! Roger, you didn't tell Gilbert that you'd brought the flowers for *me*?

Roger Oh, no.

Shirley Thank goodness for that! He might have been suspicious.

Roger Oh, I think he was far more concerned about the cleaning lady.

Shirley The one with the legs?

Roger Oh, you've seen them?

Shirley I certainly have!

Roger (*reflectively*) She seemed to be rather upset that she wasn't at home in Düsseldorf with her mother ... (*He sits on the sofa, concerned about Helga's mother*)

Shilrey glances anxiously towards the stairs, then goes to sit beside him

Shirley I wish you hadn't just turned up here without letting me know ...

Roger Well ... with Gilbert in Düsseldorf and Jane at her Old Girls' Reunion, it seemed an ideal opportunity to see you again ...

Shirley But why didn't you telephone me? Make an arrangement like we *usually* do?

Roger I wanted to surprise you ...

Shirley (*regretfully*) If only you'd stayed at home ...

Roger Why?

Shirley Because last night I didn't go to my aerobics class. I went to *your* house to see *you*!

Roger (*staring at her in astonished disbelief*) You didn't!

Shirley Well ... with Gilbert in Düsseldorf and Jane ... somewhere else ... *I* thought it was an ideal opportunity, too! So I found your spare key in the greenhouse where you always leave it, and let myself in.

Roger And I wasn't there?

Shirley No.

Roger Oh, damn ...!

Shirley So *I* slept the night in *your* house ...

Roger And *I* slept the night in *your* house ...!

Shirley ⎱
Roger   ⎰ *(together; miserably)* Ooooh ...!

Mark returns from the dining-room, carrying the tray on which are now the dirty dishes from dinner

Mark Oh, good! Shirley's looking after you. *(He chuckles)* The neighbours are very friendly in Little Bendon.

Shirley *(apprehensively)* Have you two met, then?

Mark Oh, yes. He was here just now. We had quite a conversation!

Shirley *(quickly going to Mark)* Aren't you going to take those things into the kitchen? Roger doesn't want to stare at fish bones in the middle of his coffee! *(She urges him towards the kitchen)*

Roger I didn't *get* any coffee ...

Mark Is that his name? Roger?

Shirley Yes.

Mark He told you that, did he?

Shirley It's not a secret, is it?

Mark Well, he didn't tell *me*.

Roger *(bristling a little)* I'm not in the habit of getting on to first name terms with total strangers!

Mark Ah! You mean Shirley *isn't* a total stranger?

Shirley Mark! Do go and have your breakfast! The scrambled eggs will be ruined!

Shirley pushes Mark into the kitchen and closes the door

Roger I can't think why you invited *him* to dinner ...!

Shirley I didn't! I wasn't here last night, so why should I invite anyone to dinner?

Roger Well, he *came* here ...

Shirley Yes ...

Roger So he must have thought he was going to have dinner with *someone* ...

Shirley Well, it wasn't me! *(She goes to him urgently)* Look — the fog's cleared, so you really ought to get dressed and go home! *(She pulls him to his feet and urges him towards the stairs)*

Roger *(miles away, deep in thought)* You know ... Gilbert said an extraordinary thing last night ...

Shirley Did he?

Roger He said that *Jane* had been here.

Shirley J-Jane? (*She glances anxiously towards the kitchen*)

Roger Yes.

Shirley (*assuming surprise*) Your Jane?

Roger Yes ...

Shirley But she was at her Old Girls' Reunion!

Roger Perhaps it was cancelled? They often are. If two or three of the Old Girls drop dead, they cancel the dinner. Out of deference.

Shirley Oh, no! I'm sure they're still alive and kicking! Gilbert must have been mistaken. Jane couldn't possibly have been here.

Roger Well, I hope not ... (*Amused*) Just imagine if I'd turned up here — to see *you* — and had come face-to-face with my wife!

Shirley Yes — that would have been awful ...!

Gilbert (*off; upstairs*) Come on, Helga! Don't hang about!

Shirley and Roger leap apart

Gilbert comes downstairs with a very reluctant Helga. She is now wearing Gilbert's long raincoat, which is buttoned up at the neck

Shirley and Roger stare at her in surprise. Gilbert does not yet see Roger

Shirley (*to Helga*) Do you find it very cold in here?

Helga (*disgruntled*) No! I am very warm! (*She glares at Gilbert*)

Shirley Then why are you wrapped up like that?

Gilbert (*hastily*) Because she's not staying here! She's going home! Off down the road and away! And it may be warm in here, but it's bloody freezing outside!

Roger You never brought my breakfast in bed.

Gilbert (*turning and seeing Roger for the first time*) Good God! I'd forgotten all about you!

Roger (*smiling benignly*) I was waiting for you up there for ages. Kept thinking, any minute now he'll be through the door with my two lightly boiled eggs.

Gilbert Well, you can have some coffee!

Shirley (*alarmed*) No, he can't!

Gilbert Why not?

Shirley Er ... Mark's out there having his breakfast.

Gilbert That doesn't mean he can monopolize the coffee pot. (*To Roger*) It's a bit of a full house here this morning, I'm afraid.

Shirley (*peering at Helga's very long raincoat*) Do you always wear such a very long coat when you go out cleaning?

Helga It is not my coat!

Gilbert Yes, it is!

Shirley It looks more like Gilbert's coat ...

Helga Yes, it is!

Gilbert No, it isn't! It's *her* coat! (*He turns to Roger again, anxious to change the subject*) How long have been down here, then?

Roger Oh, only a few minutes.

Gilbert (*chuckling secretly*) Have you had a word with Jane ...?

Roger Not yet. I'll telephone her when I've had my breakfast.

Gilbert (*puzzled*) Telephone her?

Shirley (*going hastily to Roger*) Come on, Roger! You must be dying to look at the garden! (*She drags him towards the garden*)

Gilbert He can't go into the garden dressed like that! What would the neighbours think? Anyway, he hasn't had his breakfast yet. (*To Roger*) We'll get Jane to cook you some eggs.

Roger (*smiling; sagely*) Oh, I'll be far too hungry if I wait till I get home. (*He chuckles at his own humour*)

Gilbert (*puzzled again*) You don't have to wait. You can have your breakfast here!

Roger Well, that would be preferable. Stoke up for the journey, eh? If Shirley doesn't mind.

Gilbert Oh, all right, then — *Shirley* can do it! (*To Shirley*) Two lightly boiled eggs for Roger. (*To Roger*) How long do you like them? Three and a half minutes?

Roger Three and half from boiling.

Shirley Right! You come and wait in the dining-room.

She drags Roger towards the dining-room

Gilbert He doesn't want to sit all alone in the dining-room for three and a half minutes from boiling.

Shirley He's got to have time for grace, hasn't he?

She pushes Roger into the dining-room and closes the door abruptly

Gilbert (*turning to Helga; keen to be rid of her*) Well, off you go, then!
Don't hang about here. (*To Shirley*) I've explained everything to Helga
and she quite understands.

Helga What are you talking about?

Shirley (*to Helga*) I'll ask Mrs Capstick about the stairs, but she's never
complained to *me* about them. Last Thursday she seemed to be going up
and down like a mountain goat.

Helga (*puzzled*) But I thought *you* were Mrs Capstick ...

Shirley Yes. I know you did. And I wasn't very flattered.

Gilbert Come on, Helga! I thought you were in a hurry to go — !

Helga No! *You* are in a hurry to *make* me go! (*She turns back to Shirley*)
If you are not Mrs Capstick, who are you?

Gilbert (*wildly*) It's too late now for introductions! You're just leaving,
so there's no point in getting to know anybody!

Shirley Didn't he tell you about me? Oh, Gilbert — I am disappointed.
(*To Helga*) I'm the lady you would have been working for if Mrs
Capstick hadn't been able to manage the stairs.

Helga You mean — you ...?

Shirley Yes. I'm Gilbert's wife.

Helga looks appalled. A dreadful pause

Gilbert (*erupting into life*) Well? Aren't you going to say how-do-you-
do?!

Helga goes to Shirley and they shake hands solemnly

Helga How do you do ...

Shirley Not nearly as well as *you* do, I'm sure! What a good thing
Gilbert's plane was cancelled, because I wasn't going to be here last
night. Oh, but I expect you already knew that?

Helga (*meekly*) You go to aerobics ...

Shirley However did you guess? So if Gilbert hadn't been here you would
have had to stay outside in your car until the fog had lifted. And all to
get a job as a cleaning lady.

Helga (*starting to cry*) I am *not* a cleaning lady ...

Shirley No. I didn't think you were somehow. (*She turns to look icily at Gilbert*)

Gilbert (*shifting uncomfortably*) I ... I must have misunderstood ...

Shirley You certainly did!

Gilbert It wasn't my fault! She ... she's German! I didn't understand what she was saying. And I couldn't leave her standing out there in the fog, could I?

Helga (*tearfully*) I am having a horrible time ...!

Shirley (*crying also*) So am I ...!

Gilbert (*instantly bursting into noisy tears himself*) So am I ...!

Helga (*to Gilbert*) I do not know why you treat me so badly. Last night I have aperitif and no afters, this morning you are angry with me for leaving toast crumbs under the duvet, you force me to wear a long coat to go home in — and then you tell your wife that I am a cleaning lady! (*She moves away in tears*)

Shirley Yes, Gilbert!

Gilbert What do you mean, "Yes, Gilbert"?

Shirley Why did you make her wear a long coat to go home in?

Gilbert I told you — it's cold outside!

Shirley It's not to hide something underneath, is it? Don't tell me she hasn't got any clothes on! (*She goes to Helga*) Come on, Helga ...

Slowly, and with a defiant look at Gilbert, Helga unbuttons the long raincoat and takes it off, revealing the Lufthansa uniform she is wearing underneath. Gilbert wishes he were a million miles away. Shirley turns to Gilbert with a smile that could slice bacon

Shirley Oh, Gilbert — why didn't you say so in the first place?

Gilbert Sorry?

Shirley When your plane was grounded, I didn't realize that you'd offered the pilot a bed for the night.

Gilbert She's not the pilot!

Shirley Then what is she? No, perhaps you'd better not answer that.

Helga I am an air hostess! (*She throws the coat at Shirley*)

Shirley Does that mean that you do up in the air what other hostesses do down on the ground?

Helga (*tearfully*) I am not happy here! I am going home ...!

She runs out into the garden, crying noisily

Gilbert *Now* see what you've done!

Shirley (*throwing the coat at him*) I haven't done *anything*! So ... you and Helga were both going to Düsseldorf on the same flight to visit her mother?

Gilbert Of course we weren't!

Shirley But you *were* travelling Lufthansa?

Gilbert They do have more than one plane! (*He tries to ingratiate himself*) Look, Shirley — there's a perfectly simple explanation ——

Shirley And you're trying to think of it?

Gilbert And I'm trying to — No! You don't really think that I'd bring a sexy young air hostess back here for a bit of hanky-panky in the fog while you were out at your aerobics class?

Shirley You might!

Gilbert Anyway, you're a fine one to talk!

Shirley (*nervously*) What do you mean?

Gilbert What about *your* guilty secret?

Shirley I didn't think you knew about that ...

Gilbert What?

Shirley (*quickly*) I haven't got a guilty secret!

Gilbert You and Mister Dinner Jacket!

Shirley (*relieved*) Oh — *him* ...

Gilbert You invited him to dinner when you thought I was safely out of the way in Düsseldorf!

Shirley No, I didn't!

Gilbert Well, he's here, isn't he? He didn't just turn up out of the blue!

Shirley But it wasn't to have dinner with *me*!

Gilbert Then who was it to have dinner with? Mrs Capstick?!

Shirley I wasn't going to tell you, Gilbert, because I knew you'd disapprove, but if you really want to know (*she casts a quick glance towards the kitchen*) — he came to have dinner with Jane!

Gilbert stares at her blankly for a moment

Gilbert Jane?

Shirley Yes.

Gilbert The Jane out there?

Shirley Yes.

Gilbert But Jane doesn't live here.

Shirley No.

Gilbert You and I live here.

Shirley Yes.

Gilbert Does Jane usually give dinner parties in other people's houses?

Shirley (*looking sheepish*) I lent it to her.

Gilbert You lent our house to Jane to have a liaison with a motor-cyclist in a dinner jacket?

Shirley Yes ...

Gilbert You sound as if you've turned into one of those French mesdames with a red light in Montmartre.

Shirley I didn't want you to know! I knew you'd be angry!

Gilbert (*calmly*) I'm *not* angry.

Shirley (*surprised*) No. You're not, are you?

Gilbert (*starting to chuckle*) So last night, Jane and her husband *and* her boyfriend were all here together?

Shirley Yes ...!

Gilbert And now *she's* in the kitchen with — ?

Shirley Yes ...

Gilbert And her husband's in the — ?

Shirley Yes!

Gilbert laughs loudly

Gilbert! I knew I shouldn't have told you ...

Gilbert But doesn't Roger know that his wife's here?

Shirley No, of course he doesn't! And *she* doesn't know that *he's* here!

Roger comes out of the dining-room, smiling patiently

Roger I say, those eggs are going to be awfully hard if they're still boiling.

Gilbert tries to control his laughter. Roger looks puzzled. Shirley glares at Gilbert

Shirley (*crossing to Roger*) Oh, I'm so sorry! We've been having a long discussion with the cleaning lady — well, she *was* the cleaning lady — or we thought she was the cleaning lady — but she's not. Not anymore. Now she's an air hostess. Isn't that nice?

Roger (*delighted*) Oh, good! I'm sure that's much more interesting for her. Travelling from place to place, seeing the world. Meeting new people ... (*He smiles, happy for Helga*)

Gilbert So I'm afraid Shirley quite forgot about your lightly boiled eggs.

Shirley I'll go and see to them now.

Roger Three and a half from boiling.

Shirley I'll remember.

Roger is about to sit down, but Shirley grabs his arm and pulls him up again

So would you — er — ?

Roger Wait in the dining-room?

Shirley What a good idea!

Roger (*to Gilbert*) It's a bit like hide-and-seek, isn't it?

He smiles innocently and disappears back into the dining-room

Shirley closes the door abruptly after him. Gilbert is chuckling, enjoying the situation enormously

Shirley (*going to him; furiously*) Now, Gilbert, whatever happens, don't let Jane know that I told you about last night.

Gilbert Why not? (*He collapses on to the sofa, laughing*)

Shirley Well, she'd be so embarrassed, wouldn't she?

Gilbert That's the least of her problems! She's going to have a hell of a surprise when she finds out that her husband's here! (*He laughs again*)

Shirley Gilbert, it's not funny!

Gilbert Oh yes, it is!

Shirley We've got to keep them apart.

Gilbert Oh, no! Don't spoil the fun. I'm longing to see her face when they meet! (*He wipes his eyes*)

Shirley Gilbert!

Gilbert Yes, darling?

Shirley (*severely*) You are going — to help me — keep them apart!

Gilbert (*still laughing*) Oh no, I'm not ...!

Shirley Oh yes, you are! (*With a sweet smile*) Don't forget — you still haven't explained how that air hostess came to be here. (*She heads for the kitchen*)

Gilbert (*stopping laughing*) Haven't I?

Jane comes out of the kitchen

Jane He's really enjoying his breakfast. He's got the most enormous appetite this morning.
Gilbert Even more than last night?

Shirley gives him a severe look

Jane Sorry?
Gilbert Surely he must have had something last night?
Jane How should *I* know?
Gilbert Driving around on a motorbike in the fog is bound to make anyone a bit peckish. He must have been starving! Don't tell me he didn't get anything? (*He tries to control his mirth*)

Shirley grabs Jane and urges her towards the hall

Shirley Now you've given Mark his breakfast don't you think you ought to be going?
Jane (*surprised by Shirley's urgency*) There's no hurry, is there?
Shirley Yes, there is! And you must keep your voice down.
Jane (*unable to think why*) Why?
Shirley (*unable to say why*) I ... I've got the most dreadful headache.

Gilbert explodes with laughter again. Jane is surprised, but tends to Shirley

Jane Oh Shirley — I am sorry. It was probably the fog.
Gilbert You might at least have offered to cook him a small snack last night. Beans on toast. Something like that. (*He laughs*)
Jane (*bewildered by his mirth*) Why should I?
Gilbert Well, as you were both staying the night you should have given him *some*thing before he went to bed! (*This remark amuses him greatly*)
Jane Well, I didn't!
Gilbert After all, you did seem to be getting on pretty well together.
Jane I was only being polite!
Shirley Jane! Please — remember my headache ...!

Jane Oh — sorry.

Gilbert (*to Shirley; enjoying himself*) Mark even insisted on taking her home. Offered her a ride on his pillion. If the fog hadn't come down, God knows what would have happened!

Jane Gilbert!

Shirley Ooh! (*She clutches her head in apparent pain*)

Jane Oh — sorry, Shirley. (*She lowers her voice*) Gilbert — I'm a happily married woman.

Gilbert Yes. I know ...! (*He laughs and looks towards the dining-room*)

Shirley Jane, I really think you ought to go! You must have things to do at home, surely? What about the shopping? It's Saturday. Sainsbury's is always packed on Saturday!

Jane Yes, you're right — perhaps I'd better go. (*She gives Gilbert a look*) I'll just fetch my handbag. I think I left it in the dining-room. (*She sets off towards the dining-room*)

Shirley (*running round to intercept her*) No! You can't go in there!

Jane (*astonished*) Why not?

Shirley It's ... it's dusty.

Jane I'm only going to fetch my handbag. I'm not going to run my finger over the surfaces. (*She starts to go*)

Shirley (*intercepting her again*) It's not in there!

Jane How do you know?

Shirley I do! And it isn't! Is it, Gilbert?

Gilbert (*wickedly*) Well, there's *something* of hers in there ...

Shirley (*glaring at him, furiously*) Yes, but it's not her handbag!

Gilbert Isn't it?

Shirley You know very well it isn't!

Jane cannot understand what is going on

Gilbert Ah! No — no, it isn't, is it? (*He goes to Jane*) I mean, how on earth could your handbag get into the dining-room if you haven't been dining? (*He smiles with heavy suspicion*) Or *were* you dining last night, after all?

Jane N-no! Of course I wasn't!

Shirley I think I saw it upstairs!

Jane Did you?

Shirley In the bathroom! So why don't you go up and get it? And then you really must get off home!

Jane Yes. You're right. I will. I'll just get my handbag and then I'll be off. (*She starts to go, and then looks back at them*) After all, Roger must be wondering where I am.

She disappears upstairs

Gilbert laughs again

Shirley (*glaring at him*) You really are dreadful!

Roger comes in from the dining-room

Roger I think tea would be rather nice. If it's no trouble.

Gilbert and Shirley look at him blankly for a moment

Gilbert Sorry?
Roger With my eggs. I always think tea suits boiled eggs better than coffee.
Gilbert Yes, of course. No bother at all. (*To Shirley*) Roger's eggs will be ready soon, won't they, darling?
Shirley Oh — yes — yes, of course!
Gilbert I should jolly well hope so.
Roger (*deep in thought*) I suppose it's a bit too early, isn't it?
Gilbert Too early for eggs?
Roger No, no — to telephone Jane.

Gilbert and Shirley exchange a hectic look

Shirley Oh, yes! It is! Much too early! She'll still be in bed!
Roger Well, perhaps I'll leave it till after I've had my breakfast.
Shirley Yes — I think you should ...!
Roger But then I'd *better* call her. After all, she must be wondering where I am ...

He disappears back into the dining-room and closes the door

Gilbert (*grinning at Shirley*) You'd better make a start on those eggs. Poor old Roger must be getting faint from hunger! (*He dissolves into laughter again*)

Shirley All right — but keep Jane out of the dining-room!

She races into the kitchen

Helga returns from the garden. Gilbert's laughter stops abruptly

Gilbert I thought you'd gone!
Helga My car won't start.
Gilbert Oh, my God ...!
Helga It must have got fog into the sparkling plugs.
Gilbert Sparking!
Helga Yes. You will give me a push?
Gilbert Are you mad?
Helga Why not? You cannot be tired. You slept all night on the sofa. (*She moves closer to him*) Oh, liebling ... You did not come to my room ...
Gilbert Of course I didn't! (*He looks nervously towards the kitchen*)
Helga I thought you wanted to?
Gilbert Of course I did! (*He lowers his voice*) But I couldn't! The place was full of people.
Helga I came downstairs to find you ...
Gilbert You didn't!
Helga But you were snorkling on the sofa.
Gilbert What?
Helga Fast asleep. Snorkling.
Gilbert Snoring!

Helga giggles, which irritates Gilbert

Helga You do not look very sexy when you are snorkling ...
Gilbert Snoring!
Helga Your lips go (*she demonstrates*) — like a horse. (*She giggles*)
Gilbert (*trying to retain his dignity*) Have you quite finished? Look — you can't stay here!
Helga But I cannot start my car. (*She moves closer to him again*) Why don't we go upstairs and pretend that we have just had our aperitif?
Gilbert Helga — my wife is in the kitchen! And there are people in various rooms having breakfast. You've got to go!
Helga (*sulking a little*) Well — do *you* know about my sparkling plugs?

Gilbert Sparking! Snoring. Sparking. OK? Right — I'll have a look. (*He makes to go*)

Helga Because if we cannot start my car, I will have to stay here with *you* ...

Gilbert Oh, no, you won't!

Mark comes out of the kitchen and sees Helga in her uniform

Mark Good God! It's the police!

Helga I am *not* the police!

Mark Oh, it's you! I didn't recognize you with your clothes on. Aren't you a little overdressed for a cleaning lady?

Helga I am *not* a cleaning lady!

Mark (*turning to Gilbert*) You told me she was a cleaning lady who worked very well in the bedrooms.

Gilbert Well, everybody makes mistakes!

Mark So what was she doing here last night?

Gilbert None of your damn business.

Mark (*to Helga*) Are you a traffic warden?

Helga No, I am *not* a traffic warden! I am an air hostess!

Mark But there's no airport for miles.

Gilbert She had to make a forced landing in the fog.

Mark What about the others?

Gilbert What others?

Mark The other members of her crew. The pilot and all that. She didn't have the whole plane to herself, did she?

Gilbert Well, they ... they got separated.

Mark Separated?

Gilbert It was foggy! And dark! They ... they lost track of each other. They're probably spread all over the place now — in different houses throughout the neighbourhood.

Mark (*going to Helga*) Well, *you* struck lucky, then, didn't you?

Helga What?

Mark You got the champagne!

Helga (*unhappily*) Yes. But no afters ...

Gilbert (*to Mark; urgently*) Isn't it time you put your trousers on and went home?

Mark All right! I'm going! (*He smiles triumphantly*) Jane's been cooking me breakfast.

Gilbert Yes, I know ...! (*He chuckles*)

Mark Which is more than she's done for you!

Gilbert Oh, that's all right. Shirley'll do me some bacon, eventually.

Mark Do you usually have your breakfast cooked by the neighbours?

Gilbert Look — will you please get dressed and go!

Mark Very well. But if *you're* staying for breakfast, I shall take Jane with me!

Gilbert Oh, good. That'll be a help.

Mark goes off upstairs with a determined tread

Helga Who is ... Jane?

Gilbert (*impatiently*) You remember — you met her last night!

Helga Oh, yes. (*Puzzled*) So that man — he came to have dinner with your wife — and now he is going off with *another* lady?

Gilbert Helga ... this is no time to discuss other people's morals.

He drags her towards the garden

Helga Where are we going?

Gilbert To look at your sparkling plugs.

They go into the garden

Shirley comes out of the kitchen, carrying a tray with two boiled eggs, some bread and butter and a small pot of tea. She looks about furtively and goes towards the dining-room

Jane reappears with her handbag, talking as she comes downstairs

Jane You were right, Shirley. It was in the bathroom.

Shirley continues walking, but makes a circular detour around the armchair, away from the dining-room. Jane arrives, and is surprised to find Shirley with the two boiled eggs on a tray

Where are you going with those?

Shirley (*blankly*) Sorry?

Jane Two boiled eggs.

Shirley Ah. Yes. I ... I thought someone might like them. It is breakfast time, after all.

Jane But Mark's already eaten.

Shirley Well, I expect I'll think of somebody ... (*Whispering urgently*) You really must go!

Jane Yes — all right! I'm on my way.

Jane starts to go towards the hall. Relieved, Shirley sets off towards the dining-room again. Jane stops and returns

Oh, Shirley ——
Shirley Aaaah!

Shirley automatically circles away around the armchair again

Jane Gilbert doesn't *know* about Mark and me, does he? You didn't tell him?

Shirley Whatever gave you that idea?

Jane Well, he was behaving very strangely just now, wasn't he? All that laughing.

Shirley I expect he was hungry. Ah! Perhaps *he'd* like these eggs!

Jane I doubt it. He's outside with his head under Helga's bonnet.

Shirley I thought she'd gone!

Jane No. She's still here. And wearing a uniform! I think she must have joined the fire brigade.

Shirley (*urgently*) Goodbye, then, Jane!

Jane I may as well wait until Mark's ready. Then we can go together.
Shirley No!

Jane (*surprised by her tone*) What?

Shirley Go! *Now*!

Jane It sounds very urgent.

Shirley It is! You'll never get into Sainsbury's car park if you don't go now.

Jane is unable to understand the urgency about Sainsbury's car park, but relents

Jane Oh, all right, then. I'll just get my coat.

She goes into the hall, leaving her handbag behind on the sofa

Shirley races out into the dining-room with the boiled eggs. After a moment she runs back in again and resumes her previous position, only without the tray

Jane returns with her coat on

Right! I'm off then, Shirley — (*she stops, puzzled, noticing something is different*) What have you done with the eggs?
Shirley Oh, I ... I put them in the dining-room.
Jane You usually have breakfast in the kitchen.
Shirley Well — so many guests — it's a special occasion! So if anyone feels peckish we'll know that there are two lightly boiled eggs in the dining-room. (*She urges Jane on her way abruptly*) Goodbye, Jane! Off you go!
Jane Yes — right. Goodbye, Shirley (*she embraces her*) — and thanks for trying last night.
Shirley It was my pleasure.
Jane I'm glad it was *someone's*!

She gives a wan smile and goes despondently into the hall

Shirley (*sighing with relief*) One gone, one to go ...!

She runs upstairs at high speed

Jane returns wearily, talking as she comes in

Jane Oh, dear. Now I've left my *handbag* behind ...

Jane stops, surprised to see that Shirley has disappeared so quickly. She shrugs, picks up her handbag and is just about to go again when ...

The dining-room door opens and Roger looks out

Roger Have you got any salt?

They both see each other and freeze, astonished and alarmed

Jane Roger ...!

Roger (*smiling stupidly and nodding*) Yes ...

Jane W-what are *you* doing here?

Roger Having two lightly boiled eggs.

Jane But ... *why*?

Roger I didn't get any dinner last night, so I'm a bit peckish this morning.

Jane (*alarmed*) You ... you mean you've been here *all night*?!

Roger Oh, yes. That's why I took my trousers off.

Jane (*anxiously*) Which ... room were you in?

Roger Top of the stairs, turn left.

Jane With all the jumble ...

Roger Sorry?

Jane (*trying to appear casual*) Did you ... hear anybody in the night? Knocking on doors?

Roger No. I slept like a log.

Jane Oh, good ...!

Roger *Was* there somebody knocking on doors?

Jane I don't know! I just wanted to be sure you'd had a good night's sleep. You know what you're like in a strange bed.

Roger Well, I think I'll just —— (*he starts to move towards the kitchen, anxious to escape*)

Jane Roger ——

He stops

—— why did you come here last night?

Roger (*nervously*) Why? Er ... well, I — I ... Do you mind if I just get the salt?

He hastens into the kitchen

Jane remains rooted to the spot, dazed

Roger returns with the salt and holds it aloft, well pleased

Salt! (*He sets off, hastily, towards the dining-room*)

Jane You said you were staying at home to watch the football.

Roger They lost, three-nil, so I went out for a drive. It was such a *lovely* evening ...

Jane It was foggy!

Roger Ah — yes — but that was later! After I went out. And that's why
I came here.

Jane But you've never *met* Gilbert.

Roger No. (*He smiles*) Funny chap, isn't he?

Jane He must have been very surprised to see you.

Roger Yes. He was rather. Mind you, I think he had his hands full with
the cleaning lady. Luckily I arrived before he went to bed. Otherwise he
might not have heard the bell!

Jane But ... *why*?

Roger Well, the bedrooms are upstairs and the bell's out in the ——

Jane Why did you *come* here?

Roger Look ... can we talk about this in a minute? I don't want my eggs
to go cold. Not when Shirley's taken the trouble to cook them. And
they're just right! Three and a half from boiling. (*He starts to go, then
stops and looks back at her*) You've just *arrived*, I take it?

Jane (*blankly*) What?

Roger Well, you've still got your coat on.

Jane (*looking down at her coat; realizing gratefully*) Oh ... er ... yes! Yes,
I — I just popped in for breakfast! (*She smiles, happy with her salvation*)

Roger Well, I can recommend the eggs. (*He starts to go, but again turns
back*) How was it last night?

Jane Er ... sorry?

Roger The Old Girls' Reunion.

Jane Oh — that! Great ...

Roger (*with a smile*) Shirley *said* Gilbert must have been mistaken.

He goes into the dining-room, closing the door behind him

*As Roger disappears, Shirley comes racing downstairs, carrying the
empty champagne bottle and heading angrily for the garden. She stops
in surprise when she sees Jane*

Shirley I thought you'd gone!

Jane I wish I had ...!

Shirley (*grimly*) You'll never believe what I found up there!

Jane And *you'll* never believe what I found down *here* ...!

Shirley Look at this! (*She brandishes the empty bottle*)

Jane Roger's in the dining-room!

Shirley freezes, the bottle aloft, and stares at Jane

Shirley What?

Jane Eating your boiled eggs.

Shirley I told you not to go in there!

Jane I didn't. He came out, looking for salt.

Shirley Really? I could have sworn I put some on the tray ...

Jane (*after a nervous glance towards the dining-room*) Why didn't you *tell* me my husband was here?

Shirley I didn't think you'd want to know!

Jane He's been here all night!

Shirley (*ruefully*) Yes, I know ...

Jane He might have seen me on the landing — knocking on other people's doors!

Shirley It's your own fault! You said he was staying at home last night.

Jane He changed his mind.

Shirley (*ruefully*) Yes — I know ...!

Jane I can't think why he came *here*.

Shirley No — neither can I!

Jane I mean, he'd never met Gilbert, and he's got nothing in common with *you*.

Shirley (*agreeing too enthusiastically*) No! Of course he hasn't! Anyway, I was at my aerobics.

Jane We'll ask him! (*She starts to go*)

Shirley grabs her as she passes and pulls her back

Shirley No! I wouldn't do that!

Jane Why not?

Shirley Well, we don't want to make a scene, do we? Not when he's having his breakfast. Besides, he might ask you what *you* were doing here last night.

Jane Oh, no! *He* thinks I've just arrived.

Shirley (*puzzled*) What?

Jane Well ... (*She indicates her coat*)

Shirley You mean he doesn't know that you were here last night?

Jane (*with a big smile*) No!

Shirley What a bit of luck!

Jane So, whatever happens, we mustn't let him talk to Mark.

Shirley Why not?

Jane Well, you know what men are like when they start talking. Things
... come out.

Shirley Do they?

Jane Of course they do! So we've got to keep Mark out of the way!

Gilbert and Helga come in from the garden

Gilbert It's no good! We'll have to ring the A A. (*To Helga*) I thought if
you worked for Lufthansa you'd know all about engines.

Helga I am an air hostess! I serve the drinks. I do not drive the plane ...!
(*She cries*)

Gilbert Oh, God — now she's crying again!

Shirley Perhaps she needs some more champagne? (*She gives Gilbert a
steely look*)

Helga (*cheering up at once*) Ooh — ja! Danke!

Gilbert What?

Shirley Where do you think I found this? (*She waves the empty bottle at
him*)

Gilbert I — I — I've no idea ...!

Shirley It was in our bedroom! And empty!

Gilbert I — I can't think how it came to be there.

Helga *I* can! (*She starts to cry again*) It was our aperitif ...! (*She sits on
the sofa*)

Gilbert glares at her

Shirley Oh, how nice, Gilbert — champagne for you and the cleaning
lady.

Helga I am *not* the cleaning lady!

Shirley Sorry. I keep forgetting.

Jane You didn't manage to get home last night, then, Helga?

Gilbert (*glaring at her*) I thought you were leaving!

Jane I've been talking to *Roger*!

Gilbert You mean you've seen him?

Jane Yes!

Gilbert (*sulking*) Oh, blast! And I missed it ...

Shirley gives him a hard look

Jane Why didn't you tell me he was here last night?

Gilbert He asked me not to.

Jane What?

Gilbert It didn't seem to crop up in the conversation!

Jane What *we* want to know is why Roger came here at all. Don't we, Shirley?

Shirley Well, *you* do. I'm not bothered ...

Gilbert He was lost in the fog!

Jane But why did he end up *here*?

Shirley Does it matter?

Jane Of course it matters! Did he tell you, Gilbert?

Gilbert Well, I didn't ask him, did I? It was none of my business why he came — (*he stops as he has a sudden idea*) Ah! Yes! (*He chuckles happily*) Jane ... would you take Helga into the kitchen and give her a cup of coffee?

Helga I do not want coffee ...

Gilbert Well, what *do* you want?

Shirley I wouldn't ask her that ...!

Helga More champagne!

Gilbert We haven't got any! Ring the A A, will you, Jane?

Jane I don't think they sell champagne.

Gilbert Helga's car won't start! And I want a word with my wife — in private!

Jane Oh, very well. (*To Shirley; quietly*) Keep an eye out for Mark. Come along, Helga!

She grabs Helga by the arm and leads her hastily out into the kitchen

Shirley looks at Gilbert coldly and holds up the champagne bottle

Shirley Well, Gilbert? What about this?

Gilbert laughs nervously, takes the bottle away from her and leads her to the sofa

Gilbert Darling ... things are never quite what they seem.

Shirley (*assuming surprise*) Really, darling?

Gilbert Oh, no.

They sit on the sofa. Gilbert carefully puts the bottle out of her reach and then looks around furtively

    I ... I couldn't tell you this before ...

Shirley Because you hadn't thought of it?

Gilbert Because I hadn't — No! Because I didn't think you'd find out.

Shirley But now I have.

Gilbert Well ... you *think* you have.

Shirley I *know* I have! Champagne in our bedroom with an air hostess seems pretty conclusive to me!

Gilbert Ah! But only on the surface. (*He gives another look around*) Shirley — I know you'll find this difficult to believe — but I slept down here last night. (*He pats the sofa*) On this thing.

Shirley Oh — poor Gilbert ...!

Gilbert What?

Shirley You must have been so uncomfortable. Honestly, some people are so selfish!

Gilbert (*puzzled*) Sorry?

Shirley Well — you down here on the sofa — and that pretty girl from Lufthansa upstairs in our bed knocking back a bottle of champagne all on her own!

Gilbert Well ... not *exactly* on her own ...

Shirley That's what I thought! (*Furiously, she tries to grab the bottle, but he quickly prevents her*)

Gilbert No, no! I didn't mean that!

Shirley Then what *did* you mean?

Gilbert (*moving closer to her; preparing to deliver the coup de grâce*) Well — you know you and Jane were wondering why *Roger* came here last night ...

Shirley No! *I* wasn't! It's perfectly clear! He was passing here and got caught in the fog!

Gilbert (*shaking his head sagely*) Doesn't sound likely, does it?

Shirley *I* think it does ...

Gilbert Well, *I* don't!

Shirley (*apprehensively*) D-don't you?

Gilbert It wasn't by *accident* that he ended up here.

Shirley W-w-wasn't it?

Gilbert Oh, no. He ... *intended* to come here.

Shirley (*uttering a high-pitched, forced laugh*) Don't be ridiculous!

Gilbert You see those flowers?

Shirley What?

Gilbert Over here.

Shirley (*turning to look at the flowers in the vase*) Er ... yes.

Gilbert *He* brought them here.

Shirley (*overdoing her surprise*) Roger?

Gilbert Yes.

Shirley Good Lord ...!

Gilbert Exactly! He brought them here ... for *her*.

Shirley Who?

Gilbert His girlfriend!

Shirley I ... I didn't know he'd *got* a girlfriend.

Gilbert Oh, yes. Still waters run deep. And I'll tell you something else — (*he leans even closer*) she's in ... this ... house.

Shirley (*assuming that her game is up*) Oh, dear ... How — how did you guess?

Gilbert What?

Shirley About Roger and — ?

Gilbert It wasn't a matter of guessing.

Shirley Wasn't it?

Gilbert Oh, no! When you told me about lending this house to Jane to meet Mister Dinner Jacket, I ... well, I was a little embarrassed.

Shirley Why?

Gilbert Because *I* was doing the same thing!

Shirley (*puzzled*) Lending the house to Jane?

Gilbert No, no! Lending the house ... to Roger!

Shirley (*now totally lost*) But ... what for?

Gilbert So he could meet his girlfriend, of course.

Shirley Which girlfriend?

Gilbert (*with a chuckle*) You'll never guess!

Shirley No, I — I don't suppose I will ...

Gilbert Helga!

Shirley The cleaning lady?

Gilbert Air hostess.

Shirley Good heavens ...! You were right. I'd never have guessed.

Gilbert That's why I couldn't explain to you about Helga when Jane was in the room. (*He grins, feeling he has covered his tracks*)

Shirley Oh, I see ...! I didn't realize. I *am* surprised ...

Gilbert But you won't say anything to *them* about it, will you? We mustn't let Jane find out.

Shirley (*over-enthusiastically*) No — of course not!

Gilbert So ... that's all right, then, isn't it?

Shirley Yes — it certainly is ...! (*She smiles in happy relief and kisses him on the cheek*)

Mark comes downstairs. He is now wearing his dinner suit again. He sees Gilbert being kissed by Shirley

Mark I see you're getting to know the neighbours!

Gilbert Ah! You've got your clothes on again. That *is* a relief. We don't want the ladies getting over-excited, do we?

Shirley (*leaping up and racing urgently to Mark*) Mark — you really must go!

Mark points at Gilbert agressively

Mark Is *he* staying here?

Shirley Well ... yes. I suppose so.

Mark Then I'll take Jane with *me*!

Shirley No! You can't do that!

Gilbert No — her husband might object ... (*he laughs*)

Mark (*glaring at him*) I'm not leaving her here with you!

Shirley But you and Jane mustn't go together!

Mark Why not?

Roger comes in from the dining-room, feeling much better for his breakfast

Roger Very nice eggs.

Shirley (*seeing him*) Oh, my God ...!

Roger Just as I like them. (*He sees Mark in his dinner suit*) Oh — very smart. You know — I've never seen anyone wear a dinner jacket for breakfast before. I must try it sometime ...

Shirley Come on, Mark!

She pulls Mark towards the hall

It's time you were off!

Roger (*to Gilbert*) Your wife's a very good cook.
Gilbert Is she?

Mark escapes from Shirley and glares at Gilbert

Mark I don't suppose *you've* even noticed!
Gilbert (*looking a little hurt*) Well, I haven't had my breakfast yet ... (*He gets up and joins Roger*) The kitchen's rather busy this morning.
Mark (*to Roger*) *Jane* cooked your eggs, then?
Roger Oh, no. I didn't know Jane was here then.

Mark tries to work this out. Shirley looks apprehensive

Mark But I thought you said ——
Roger (*smiling benignly*) *Shirley* cooked my eggs.
Shirley (*hastily grabbing Mark again*) If you go now you'll miss the traffic!
Mark (*restraining her*) But *this* is Shirley!
Roger Yes, that's right. (*To Gilbert*) He's very quick on the uptake, isn't he?
Gilbert Yes. Remarkable brain. Moves with the speed of light.
Shirley I wish *he'd* do the same ...! (*She pulls Mark's arm again*) Come on, Mark!
Mark (*resisting*) But Shirley's a neighbour! She lives down the road!
Gilbert No, she doesn't. She lives here.
Mark In this house?
Gilbert Where do you expect? A tent in the garden?
Shirley Mark, I really think you ought to go!
Mark Wait a minute! (*He grabs Shirley and thrusts her towards Gilbert for inspection*) *This* is your wife?
Gilbert Yes. That is my wife.
Mark (*looking shattered*) I thought you were married to Jane!

Gilbert and Roger laugh together, enjoying this enormously

Gilbert No, of course I'm not! (*To Roger*) Am I?
Roger Not so far as I know!

They laugh again

Mark (*taking a tentative step towards them*) Doesn't ... this house belong to Jane?

Gilbert I hope not, or we'll have to start paying her rent!

He and Roger laugh some more

No, no — *he's* the one who's married to Jane.

Mark freezes, gazing at Roger, appalled

Mark *You?*

Roger Yes. (*He loses heart*) Well, I was at the last census.

Gilbert If you'd known that before, you'd probably never have thrown my photograph into the wastepaper basket.

He and Roger enjoy this enormously

Roger (*casually*) You ... you *know* Jane, then?

A dreadful pause

Mark Er ... what?

Roger (*to Gilbert*) He's slowing down.

Gilbert Bound to happen. He peaked too soon.

Roger (*to Mark*) *Do* you?

Mark (*blankly*) What?

Roger Know my wife.

Mark (*nervously*) Well, I ... I've *seen* her. (*To Shirley*) Haven't I? (*To Roger*) She was here. (*To Shirley*) Wasn't she? (*To Roger*) Just now. (*To Shirley*) I think ...

Shirley Yes! She popped in this morning for breakfast!

Mark Exactly! And that's when I saw her!

Roger (*thinking hard*) Wait a minute, though ...

Shirley Mark can't stay! He's in a hurry to go!

Mark Yes — I am! (*He is about to make his escape when ...*)

Jane and Helga come in from the kitchen

Jane The A A can't get here for at least two hours.

Helga (*smiling happily*) So I will have to stay here. (*She settles herself on the sofa*)

Gilbert looks alarmed. Jane sees Roger and also looks alarmed

Jane Roger!
Gilbert Helga!

Gilbert crosses hastily to Helga, and passes Jane as she crosses hastily to Roger

Jane You can't have finished your eggs already!
Gilbert You're not staying here!
Roger Yes. I have. They were delicious.
Helga But I have to wait for the A A.
Roger I can recommend Shirley as a cook.
Gilbert Well, you'll have to wait for them outside!
Shirley Oh Roger, that *is* kind of you ... (*She blows him a kiss*)
Gilbert If the A A arrive and find an empty car they'll go away again!
Mark Jane! I've just been talking to your husband ...!

Jane looks alarmed

Helga Why can't they ring the doorbell when they arrive?
Jane (*to Mark*) Well, you've got your clothes on so why don't you go home?
Gilbert You're supposed to remain with your vehicle!
Shirley Yes, Mark — there's no point in your staying here!

She gives him a hefty push and he goes flying out into the hall at high speed

Helga That is when you are out on the open road!
Roger (*pointing after Mark*) But there's something I wanted to ask him — !
Jane Roger, you've finished your eggs so go and get dressed! We must get back home before the fog comes down again!

She pushes him towards the stairs

Helga (*having heard this; to Shirley*) Is he her husband?
Shirley (*quietly*) Yes. But don't worry. She doesn't know about you. (*She winks secretively, and then grins at Gilbert*)
Helga (*puzzled*) What?

Roger looks back as Jane is pushing him towards the stairs

Roger You made a mistake last night, didn't you, Gilbert?
Gilbert (*jumping like a startled bird*) Did I? Which one was that?
Roger You said that my wife came here.
Gilbert Yes, she did.
Shirley
Jane   (*together*) No, she didn't!
Gilbert What?
Shirley She came here this morning! Don't you *remember*? (*She nods at him desperately*)
Gilbert Ah — yes — of course! It was the lady next door who came last night. Mrs Ogshot. Very nice woman. Came to borrow some sugar.
Roger (*smiling contentedly*) I knew it couldn't have been Jane, because she was at her Old Girls' Reunion last night.

He goes out up the stairs

Gilbert pulls Helga up from the sofa

Gilbert Come on, Helga! You'd better go!
Helga But what about my car?
Gilbert Leave it here!
Helga But how am I going to get home?
Gilbert Roger can give you a lift.
Shirley Yes. From what you tell me, Gilbert, I'm sure he'd be delighted ... (*She grins at Gilbert*)
Jane (*puzzled*) Why should Roger be delighted?
Helga I do not want to go with Roger!
Gilbert Don't be silly! Of *course* you want to go with Roger!
Shirley (*to Helga; quietly*) It's all right. I know all about it ... (*She winks again at Helga*)

Helga looks puzzled

Gilbert Right! That's settled, then! Come on, Helga! (*He pulls her towards the garden*) You're going with Roger!

Mark returns from the hall. He is now back in his motorbike gear and is carrying his helmet

Helga (*seeing Mark*) If I *have* to go, why don't I go with Mark on his motorbike?

Gilbert (*a little jealous*) I don't think that's a very good idea!

Helga Why not, liebling? (*She crosses to take Mark's arm*) I am sure Mark will find room for me on his pillion ...

Mark Well, I ... I suppose you could squeeze up behind me ...

Gilbert She doesn't have to squeeze up behind you at all! Roger will be delighted to take her. He's got plenty of room in his car!

Shirley Darling, there's no need to get so excited.

Helga If you will not let me stay here, then I prefer for Mark to take me. (*She smiles at Mark, enjoying Gilbert's jealousy*)

Gilbert No, you don't! *Roger's* taking you!

Jane (*impatiently*) What does it matter who the hell's taking Helga? Mark's in a hurry to go!

Mark Yes, I am! (*He starts to go*)

Roger, now properly dressed, comes downstairs. He sees Mark

Roger Ah! Mark — you're still here ——

Mark Not for much longer ...

Jane Oh, Roger, you're ready! Good! We really must go! (*She tries to urge him on his way*)

Roger While I was putting on my tie I started thinking ...

Gilbert What a coincidence! *I* often do that.

Roger And there's something I don't understand ...

Jane We don't have to go into this now, do we? If we hang about here much longer the fog'll come back!

She tries to push him farther but he stands firm

Roger (*to Mark*) You told me last night that you were having dinner with Gilbert's wife only it wasn't Gilbert's wife because you just said that you thought Jane was Gilbert's wife so you must have meant that you

were having dinner with *my* wife only she was at her Old Girls'
Reunion ...

Jane Yes! Yes — I was!

Mark You must have misunderstood! I didn't mean that I was having
dinner with *Jane*!

Roger Then who *were* you having dinner with?

*A dreadful pause. Mark cannot think of a way out. Gilbert comes to the
rescue*

Gilbert Mrs Ogshot.

Everyone looks at Gilbert

Roger What?

Gilbert Didn't I tell you about Mrs Ogshot?

Roger You said she popped in to borrow some sugar.

Gilbert Well, that wasn't what she *really* popped in for.

Jane Wasn't it?

Gilbert Of course not! Mrs Ogshot's famous for it.

Roger For borrowing sugar?

Gilbert No, no! Famous for having toyboys.

Mark Toyboys?!

Roger (*turning to Mark*) So *that*'s what you are. A toyboy!

Mark Oh, no, I'm not!

Jane (*quietly*) Oh, yes, you are . . . !

Roger (*to Gilbert*) And you lend your house to Mrs Ogshot to meet
        her . . . toyboys?

Gilbert (*outraged*) Of course I don't. But *Shirley* does. (*He grins at Shirley*)

Shirley What?!

Gilbert That's why when Mrs Ogshot arrived last night and saw *me* here,
        she pretended to be coming for sugar when really she was
        coming for -

Shirley Gilbert! We don't need to go into the details.

Gilbert Don't we? Oh, what a pity. I was just getting into my stride.

Shirley (*to Mark; quietly*) If I were you, I should go *now* while the going's good ...
Mark Yes! I will!

He runs quickly out into the garden

Gilbert How very rude. He never even said, "Thank you for having me."

Gilbert's bonhomie fades a little as Helga approaches

Helga Goodbye, liebling! (*She kisses him and smiles delightfully*) I will see you on Lufthansa ...
Shirley Oh no, you won't! Next time he's travelling British Airways!

Outside Mark's motorbike starts to rev up

Helga Mark! (*As she goes*) Mark, wait for me! Mark ...!

Helga runs out into the garden

Gilbert sees Shirley's icy look and smiles nervously

Jane Well, come on, Roger! *We'd* better be off, too!

She pulls him towards the french windows

Roger You haven't had your breakfast yet.
Jane I'm not hungry!
Roger You came all this way to breakfast when you weren't hungry?
Jane I — I *was* hungry! But I've lost my appetite ...
Roger I can't think why you came here for breakfast, anyway. You don't usually do that.
Jane I ... I was lonely!
Roger Lonely?
Jane (*heavily pathetic*) Well, darling, I had been on my own *all night* in our great big empty house ...

She winks at Shirley and goes into the garden

Roger (*deep in thought again*) But Shirley, I thought *you* said that you —— ?

Shirley (*hastily*) Goodbye, Roger! (*She shakes his hand*)

Roger What?

Shirley (*pointedly*) *Goodbye*, Roger ...

Roger (*realizing*) Ah — yes! (*He turns to shake hands with Gilbert*) It was nice meeting you, Gilbert! And thanks for the use of the bedroom.

Gilbert (*with laboured innuendo for Shirley's benefit*) Anytime, Rodge — you know that ... (*He winks saucily*)

Roger looks puzzled by this and starts to go, but hesitates beside Shirley

Roger Do you *always* go to your aerobics class on a Friday night?

Shirley Oh, yes. Always on a Friday.

Roger (*smiling secretly*) I'll have to remember ...

He disappears into the garden

Gilbert looks inquiringly at Shirley. She avoids his eyes, and looks about for something

Gilbert What did he mean by that?

Shirley (*innocently*) Mean by what, darling?

Gilbert "I'll have to remember"!

Shirley (*with a vague shrug*) *I* dunno. Not to invite us to dinner on a Friday, I suppose. (*She looks about more urgently, searching for something as she did at the beginning of the play*)

Gilbert notices Shirley searching

Gilbert What are you looking for?

Shirley The bag with my leotard and things in it. I can't remember where I put it. (*She searches frantically*)

Gilbert Probably in your car.

Shirley No. I looked. (*An awful thought*) Oh, my God ... !

Gilbert What's the matter?

Shirley (*horrified*) I must have left it behind this morning!

Gilbert At Caroline's?

Shirley Er ... yes - at Caroline's ...

Gilbert Well, that's nothing to worry about. She's bound to find it, and when she does she'll ring you up and tell you.

Shirley (*anxiously*) Yes, she will, won't she? I . . . I think I'll go and have some breakfast. (*She tries to appear relaxed*) So . . . when the phone rings it'll only be Caroline, so don't you bother - I'll answer it. (*She starts to go*)

Gilbert Darling . . . ?

Shirley (*stopping*) Hmm?

Gilbert You . . . you believe what I told you about Roger and Helga, don't you?

Shirley (*returning*) Didn't you expect me to?

Gilbert Well. . . knowing how suspicious you've been, you might have thought I'd made it up.

Shirley Don't be silly, liebling! (*She kisses him lightly, just as Helga did*) Why on earth should you make up a story like that?

Gilbert Yes . . . yes - quite!

Shirley sets off towards the kitchen again

(*He chuckles, his confidence building*) After all — if Roger didn't bring those flowers for Helga, who *did* he bring them for?

Shirley (*turning and looking back at him; innocently*) Yes — exactly ...

She slides out into the kitchen

Gilbert remains for a moment, laughing to himself contentedly. Then his smile fades as he has a sudden, dawning realization

Gilbert Shirley ...? (*Then, loudly*) Shirley !

Loud music floods in as Gilbert races towards the kitchen and ——

— the CURTAIN *falls*

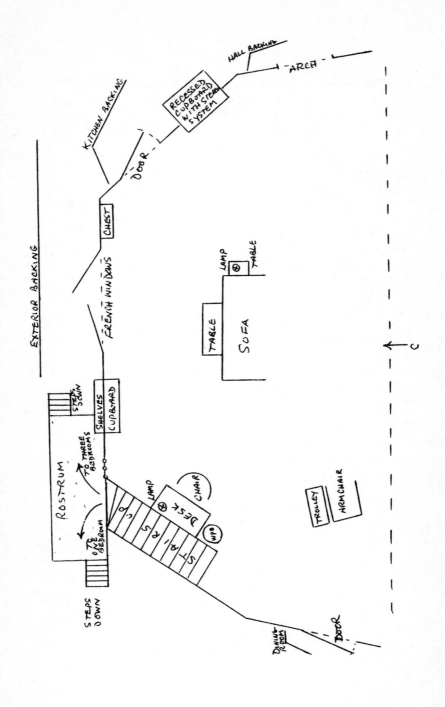

FURNITURE AND PROPERTIES LIST

ACT I

On stage: Sofa. *On it:* travel bag, towel, washbag, **Shirley's** coat, **Shirley's**
handbag containing lipstick
Sofa table. *On it:* magazines
Coffee table
Lamp (practical)
Armchair
Drinks trolley with whisky, gin, tonics and various glasses
Desk. *On it:* lamp (practical), framed photograph of Gilbert, **Jane's**
handbag containing breath freshener
Wastepaper basket
Cupboards (full)
Oak chest containing travelling rug
Stereo system
Wall telephone
Potted house plants
Curtains
Carpet

Off stage: Leotard (**Shirley**)
Plastic bag containing evening shoes (**Mark**)
Can of lager (**Jane**)
Dish of nuts (**Jane**)
2 white table napkins (**Jane** and **Mark**)
Bottle of champagne (**Gilbert**)
2 champagne flutes (**Gilbert**)
Jane's coat (**Gilbert**)
Jane's weekend bag (**Gilbert**)
Small bunch of flowers (**Roger**)

Personal: **Jane:** wrist-watch
Gilbert: latchkey, Lufthansa air ticket

ACT II

Strike: Travelling rug

Off stage: Handbag (**Shirley**)
               Mug of coffee (**Helga**)
               Plate with buttered toast (**Helga**)
               Raincoat (**Gilbert**)
               Vase (**Shirley**)
               Tray (**Mark**)
               Mug of coffee (**Shirley**)
               Dirty dinner plates and cutlery (**Mark**)
               Tray. *On it:* 2 boiled eggs in 2-stem eggcup, mug of tea, plate of bread
                   and butter (**Shirley**)
               Jane's handbag (**Jane**)
               Salt pot (**Roger**)
               Empty champagne bottle (**Shirley**)

Personal: Nil

LIGHTING PLOT

Property fittings required: two table lamps
Interior. The same scene throughout

ACT I

To open: Winter evening effect; electric lights on

Cue 1   **Jane** operates dimmer   (Page 5)
            Fade a little

Cue 2   **Jane** operates dimmer   (Page 9)
            Bring up to full

Cue 3   **Gilbert** switches off main lights   (Page 47)
            Cut main lighting

Cue 4   **Gilbert** switches off table lamp   (Page 49)
            Black-out

ACT II

To open: Dim lighting onstage with bright sunshine filtering through

Cue 5   **Shirley** draws back the curtains   (Page 50)
            Bring up full daylight effect

EFFECTS PLOT

ACT I

To open: Music

Cue 1   **Jane** reaches the foot of the stairs and moves into the room   (Page 1)
            Fade music

Cue 2   **Shirley** goes into the hall   (Page 5)
            Front door slams

Cue 3   **Jane** turns on the stereo   (Page 5)
            Burst of loud, noisy music

Cue 4   **Jane** retunes the stereo   (Page 5)
            Cut loud music; fade in romantic music

Cue 5   **Jane** turns off the stereo   (Page 8)
            Cut music

Cue 6   **Mark** and **Jane** go into the dining-room   (Page 12)
            Front door slams

Cue 7   **Gilbert** and **Mark** go into the hall   (Page 22)
            Front door slams

Cue 8   **Jane:** "What's that got to do with it?"   (Page 27)
            Back door slams

Cue 9   **Gilbert:** "Well, I had things to see to down here."   (Page 32)
            Sound of a motorbike driving off

Cue 10   **Helga** grabs **Gilbert** enthusiastically   (Page 34)
            Front doorbell rings

Cue 11   **Gilbert:** *"They'll* have rung the bell!"   (Page 34)
            Front doorbell rings

Cue 12   **Gilbert** tiptoes to the top of the stairs   (Page 48)
            Telephone rings four times

ACT II